The Islands' Rich & Famous

Sonia Hillsdon

and

Jeff Le Caudey

The Islands'
Rich and Famous

CHANNEL
ISLAND
PUBLISHING

Published in 2003 by Channel Island Publishing

Channel Island Publishing acknowledge with thanks permission to
reproduce photographs supplied by Stuart Abraham

Channel Island Publishing
Unit 3B Barrette Commercial Centre
La Route du Mont Mado, St John
Jersey, Channel Islands
JE3 4DS

Tel: 01534 860806

www.channelislandpublishing.com
email: info@channelislandpublishing.com

ISBN 0 9525659 2 7

Cover design and overall production by Simon Watkins
Page design and typesetting by Axiom Design
Photography by Stuart Abraham
Printed by The Cromwell Press, Trowbridge, Wiltshire.

Contents...

Chapter One

A Brief History

Set sail from St. Malo, head north for about 40 miles and you will find yourself approaching Les Iles Normandes. Set sail, however, from Southampton, head south for about 100 miles and you will find yourself approaching the Channel Islands. In other words, you arrive at the same group of islands in the Gulf of St. Malo with two different names, one French, the other English. This fact, together with the Islands' proximity to France and their distance from England, briefly shore up the main thread which runs through the history of the Channel Isles: over the centuries the French and English have fought each other for their possession.

The Channel Islands' first visitors walked here from France. That was about 250,000 years ago, when the sea level was much lower than it is today. They came to hunt the wild animals that roamed the grassy stretch of the continental shelf which, at that time, joined France to England. The visits of these early tourists to the tree covered hills on a rocky plateau that the Islands had become, were short. The only evidence, in fact, that they came at all is in Jersey. And there, in St Brelade, high above Ouaisné slip, tucked away up in the cliffs of Portelet common, is a cave. That cave was used by different groups of these old stone age hunters for over 150,000 years.

All they left behind were the ashes of the fires they lit to keep warm; bones of the mammoths and rhinos they caught and killed; sharp pieces of flint and stone they used to cut the animals' flesh from the bones to eat; and, sadly, the remains of at least two burials - including a tiny fragment of a child's skull. Yet that one small cave, La Cotte de St Brelade, is now renowned as one of the most important palaeolithic sites in the whole of Europe.

Our next visitors came here by boat. They needed their primitive canoes because, by about 7,000 BC, the sea level between France and England had risen and the grassy plateau between them began to divide into the separate islands we know today. These visitors left behind magnificent monuments - built to house and honour their dead.

These include megalithic remains - some still partially buried - around Herm's common; two burial chambers in Sark; the Tourgis dolmen in Alderney overlooking Clonque Bay; Le Long Rocher - Les Paysans in Guernsey, the largest standing stone in the whole of the Channel Isles; and finally, in Jersey, La Hougue Bie, possibly one of the finest neolithic monuments in Europe with its passage grave lined with sixty-four huge stones, where five men and three women were buried 5,500 years ago.

And the fighting to gain possession of the Channel Islands? It was just about to begin; at first though, only in a minor way with defensive iron age earthworks, such as those on Guernsey's Jerbourg Peninsula and Jersey's promontory fort of Le Câtel de Rozel, which would suggest that both islands had enemies that they needed to be protected against.

There were, however, no battles at all between the tribe of Gauls which had conquered the Islands about 300 BC and the Romans. Once Julius Caesar had made his conquests in France and Britain and included the islands in the Roman province of Lyonaise; the Romans virtually by-passed the Islands and left just a few of their relics in Alderney and Jersey only.

The next battle was, in fact, a spiritual one when, in the 6th century, Christian saints fought to save Islanders' heathen souls. Among the missionaries who came to convert the Islanders were St Sampson who landed in Guernsey; St Helier and St Branwalader in Jersey; while St Magloire - also known as St Mannelier - founded a monastery in Sark.

Perhaps equally important for the Islands was the expulsion, a little later, by the Frankish King of the Archbishop of Rouen to Jersey. During his seven year banishment, the Archbishop not only helped with the organisation of the Christian groups in the Islands, but he was probably also instrumental in the Islands' move from St. Sampson's diocese of Dol in Brittany to the diocese of Coutance in Normandy.

Three centuries after the coming of the Christian missionaries, the Islanders became the target of a much dreaded enemy. They were the pillaging, plundering Vikings who came every summer to murder the Islanders, burn their houses and raze their churches to the ground. These men from the north, or Norsemen as they were soon called, decided after a time, however, to over-winter in the Islands and start to farm. They began to settle and farm on the coastal strip of the continent too, just opposite the Islands' eastern coasts.

The only legacy, though, that these early Norse settlers left were place names. So we have the large islands (ey) of Alderney, Guernsey and Jersey and the small islands (hou) of Burhou, Jethou and Lihou. We also have the large rock (etac) of L'Etacq in Jersey; the strong current (raz) of Raz Island off Alderney; and land jutting out into the sea (nez) of Bec de Nez in Guernsey.

But these Norse raiders in the land we now call France were not content with just a coastal strip in the north, they dared to go further south. In 885 AD an army of Norsemen set sail up the Seine to lay siege to Paris. Besieged by such a superior force, the King of the Franks had only one recourse - to buy off the raiders.

That ransom, however, was not the end of the King's troubles. Charles learned that his subjects in Rouen were now the continual target of the Norse ruler, Rollo. Charles therefore decided that something more permanent should be done to stop the Norsemen's raids so, in 911, the important treaty of Saint Clair sur Epte was signed by Charles and Rollo. It was to have a lasting effect on all the Channel Islands.

In this treaty Rollo agreed, once and for all to stop his raiding incursions into the Frank territory; Charles, for his part agreed to give Rollo all the northern territory round Rouen. This Dukedom, given by Charles to Rollo and his followers, who were now being called Normans, was from then on known as Normandy.

The next important step was taken by Rollo's son, William Longsword. On his accession, William incorporated the Islands into his Duchy. Thus it came about that, from 933 to 1204, the Islands were ruled from Rouen in Normandy. As they were now governed in secular as well as ecclesiastical matters from Normandy, the Islanders were naturally treated as if they were Normans too.

Under the Duchy's feudal system, of which they were now a part, the Islands were divided into fiefs, each ruled by a Seigneur living in his own manor. In return for their fiefs, the Seigneurs paid their dues either in goods or in personal service to the Duke. The Seigneurs themselves were also landlords, leasing out parts of their land to tenant farmers who, in their turn, paid their dues by working in the Seigneurs' fields or mills.

The language spoken in both Normandy and the Islands was Norman-French, a version of French still spoken by some Islanders today. Their laws were the same too, based on 'Le Grand Coutumier de Normandie,' still the basis of the Islands' legal system. They lived in similar granite houses and had a love of the sea in their blood. They even looked similar in appearance, as Victor Hugo noted in 1866, with a combination of the Saxon fairness, with the proverbial ruddiness of the Norman people -

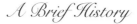

rosy cheeks and blue eyes! In 1970, the Jersey historian Balleine notes other similarities; 'The typical Jerseyman today, in his staunch independence, his self-reliance, his shrewdness at a bargain, his tremendous industry, his reticence, his thrift, is almost the exact counterpart of the Norman across the water.' But, of course, if they often have the same surnames such as de Carteret, Giffard, Malet what else would one expect?

So the Islands remained 'Les Iles Normandes' through the English reigns of Edmund, Eadred, Eadwig, Edgar, Edward the Martyr, Ethelred the Unready, Edmund Ironside, Canute, Harold I, Hardicanute, Edward the Confessor, Harold II and William I. Then William II, by his victory over Harold's forces at Hastings, united England, Normandy and Les Iles Normandes under the same Crown, with 'Les Iles' continuing to be governed from Rouen.

Then, after 273 years of Les Iles coming under Norman rule, with several of the Dukes of Normandy also being Kings of England at the same time, there came a great change. In 1202, Philippe August of France determined to become the King of Normandy as well as of the rest of France and invaded Normandy. But it was, at this time, ruled over by King John of England and also garrisoned in several strategic places by English as well as Norman troops.

It took Philippe two years to oust John from Normandy. But when, in 1204, Rouen - the centre of the Island's government - eventually surrendered to the French forces, Philippe had won and John had forever lost England's last French possession - Normandy.

It was then that Islanders were given the choice - to be governed by France or by England. They chose to remain as subjects of King John. So with all administrative matters no longer in the hands of Rouen's authorities, the self-government of the Islands, under the guidance of the English kings, gradually evolved.

First of all, in 1279, Edward I gave the Islands permission to use a public seal, bearing the Royal Arms of three leopards, for the official sealing of all their public documents. Eleven years later, separate civic heads, known as Bailiffs, were appointed by the Crown for the Bailiwicks of Guernsey - which included Alderney and Sark - and Jersey. The Bailiffs were supported in their role as Chief Magistrates by Jurats, who were elected from the ranks of the most important and wealthy Islanders but the Islands were still overseen by a Warden, appointed by the King.

Since Rollo's time the Islands had always been self-supporting and this independence continued for the two new Bailiwicks. Their laws remained Norman and at the parish level were, later, in the 15th century, to be administered by the civic head of each of the parishes, the 'Connétable' or Constable, with the help of his honorary police force.

There was, however, a new threat to be reckoned with - France was now a potential enemy, just across the water and powerful. England's King John was also keeping his eye on France and needed a strong front line against any future French invasion. So, at his command, Castle Cornet was built in Guernsey to guard England's trade routes with southern France, while Jersey's Gorey Castle - subsequently called 'Mont Orgueil' because of its lofty, proud presence opposite Normandy - was erected to defend Jersey against a French invasion. King John also ordered that one fifth part of the yearly incomes of the Islands' feudal tenants, both lay and ecclesiastical, should be raised to help towards the cost of defending the Islands.

Unfortunately, despite their cost, neither castle proved impregnable against a French attack. In the 13th century Jersey was raided and Sark invaded and occupied by French pirates.

In 1294 a French fleet attacked Jersey and, once on shore, ransacked its churches and many of its secular buildings. In the 14th century, despite the formation of a Militia and the building of Grosnez Castle and

Guernsey's Castle Cornet, both Bailiwicks suffered not only devastating French raids but also French occupation.

In 1338 a French Admiral occupied Jersey for six months. A year later Gorey Castle was attacked. Even worse befell Guernsey - it was occupied by the French from 1340 to 1345. The irony for that unfortunate Bailiwick was that, in 1341, Edward III issued a charter confirming both its customs and privileges. Then when, in 1356, Castle Cornet was again taken by the French, it was a Jersey force that had to sail to Guernsey in order to recapture the castle for their sister island.

At last, though, there seemed to be welcome news for all the vulnerable frontline Islanders. In 1360, by the Treaty of Bretegny, the French finally agreed to abandon all claims to the Channel Islands. Their good intentions, however, did not last long. Only 13 years later, the Constable of France was heading a force which not only attacked Jersey and captured Gronez Castle, but also gained possession of the inner defences of Gorey Castle as well.

Worse, though, was still to come. In 1380, France and Castile signed the Treaty of Paris. This treaty signified their agreement to invade and depopulate all the Channel Islands. This resulted in their combined forces occupying both Guernsey and Jersey for two years. Fortunately, neither island was despoiled as much as the subjugated Islanders had feared. Did they see it as some reward for their long - suffering loyalty to England when, in 1394, by the Royal Charter of Richard II, Islanders no longer had to pay the tolls and customs which were payable by the King's subjects in England?

There was certainly no let up of the French attacks on Jersey during the next century. In 1403 a fleet of ships from Brittany attacked the Island. Three years later there was another attempted invasion. This resulted in a battle in St Aubin's Bay which, unfortunately, the defenders lost, so Islanders had to pay a ransom to their attackers to retain their freedom.

During a French raid in 1454, however, the French were beaten back with such force that five hundred of their men were killed in the battle.

1461 was not, though, such a fortunate year for Jersey. Not only did the French gain possession of Gorey Castle - some thought by treachery - but they also ruled Jersey for the next seven years. It was, in the end, an Admiral of the English fleet who recovered the Island from the French. In 1468 he laid siege to Gorey Castle and its French garrison for five months until he had regained its possession and triumphantly set the King's banners fluttering from all its turrets.

It is no wonder then that, in 1483, Edward IV and Louis XI agreed that the war-weary Channel Islands should be regarded in the event of a war as neutral. It is no wonder either that English monarchs from Henry IV to Henry VII, as a mark of gratitude for the Islands' loyalty, signed charters proclaiming and conferring their privileges and liberties, recalling how nobly the Islanders had acted for the Islands' safety.

But the much smaller islands of Alderney and Sark? How had they fared since Sark had been occupied by those French pirates in the 13th century? Truth to tell, neither island had any defences to speak of, so throughout the following two centuries they both suffered cruel raids from more pirates, while Sark was so frequently occupied by the French, that often the Sarquese population fled their island and left it to their conquerors.

Indeed the French so regarded Sark as theirs that they built three small forts on it to guard the Island against a Channel Island attempt to recapture it!

Henry VIII certainly had his continental enemies on his mind when he appointed commissioners to report on the fortifications of the Channel Islands, England's first line of defence. The result was that towers were added to both Castle Cornet and Gorey Castle and, in 1542, a tower was

built at the west side of St Aubin's Bay in Jersey to safeguard the shipping moored there. Four years later a fort was built in Alderney for the greater protection of Longy Bay.

The French, however, despite any protestation to the contrary, still had their eyes on the Islands and, in 1549, after raiding Guernsey and taking Sark, the French force landed at Bouley Bay to raid Jersey. Fortunately, the Parish Companies of Jersey's Militia defeated the raiding party on the slopes of Jardin d'Olivet.

When Elizabeth I came to the throne, her charter again confirmed the Islanders' liberties, as well as reaffirming the neutrality of all the Islands, together with the seas around them. It also stated that no Islander should be cited by any form of legal process to appear before an English court. It was later agreed that all suits were to be heard by the Islanders' own Royal Courts with any appeal made solely to the English Privy Council. By Elizabeth's charter, the freedom of both Bailiwicks from all English trade restrictions and their administrative and judicial independence was upheld.

But Elizabeth was also important to the Island in other ways. In 1563 she favoured Guernsey by founding Elizabeth College, the Island's first grammar school. Two years later she gave permission to Jersey's Helier de Carteret to colonise the almost uninhabited Sark. Then, because Gorey Castle was now vulnerable to cannon fire as it had not been to bows and arrows, Paul Ivy, the Crown Engineer was sent over to plan a more impregnable castle. This time a castle to protect St Helier and Jersey's south coast. Elizabeth herself gave £500 towards the cost of building its keep. So, when Sir Walter Raleigh was made Jersey's Governor and lived in the new castle, he named it 'Fort Isabella Bellissima' in the Queen's honour. Today it is known simply as Elizabeth Castle.

Safeguarding charters and improved defences were not the only changes the Tudor monarchs brought to the Islands: there was also the disrupting dissension of the Reformation. In Henry VIII's reign, once Martin Luther had pinned his objections to certain Catholic practices on the church door in Wittenberg, the conflict between the new protesters, or Protestants, and the Catholics began. In 1528, in Normandy, the first Protestants were burnt to death for their heresy. In the second year of Edward VI's reign all the Island's chantry chapels were closed and their endowments confiscated. The Crown also ordered that all objects of superstition, such as crosses on altars and along the waysides, should be destroyed. When, a year later, the Act of Uniformity forbade the Island's rectors to use Latin and Catholic services, Jersey's States invited two Protestant clergymen from France to lead the people in the new Protestant services. In 1550, as the Islanders' first language was still French, it was arranged for the English Protestant Book of Common Prayer to be translated and printed in French especially for them.

But, interestingly, an Order to Council at the same time as ordering the use of the translated Prayer Book, also instructed Islanders to respect the ecclesiastical jurisdiction of the Bishop of Coutances as before, providing that this was not contrary to the laws of King Edward. Also that same year, commissioners were appointed to sell all confiscated church property, together with all church bells, save one left for each church, and then to hand over the proceeds to the Crown.

During Mary's brief reign, Catholic services were again allowed in the Islands' churches, but by this time, the strict influence of Calvin had reached the Islands and they kept to the simple Protestant services he had inaugurated. With Elizabeth on the throne it was a return once more to Protestantism and many Huguenots fled to the Channel Islands to avoid persecution in Catholic Europe. Some of them eventually became parish rectors and were in their new posts when the order came for all altars, fonts and benches to be taken from the churches and destroyed.

Such was the growth of Protestantism, especially Calvinism, in the Islands that, in 1564, Guernsey hosted the first United Calvinist Synod.

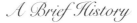

When, four years later, the Church of England brought the Islands under the jurisdiction of the Bishop of Winchester, thereby breaking their centuries long connection with the Bishop of Coutances, it meant nothing to the Calvinist Islanders - they did not believe in bishops anyway! Finally, at the Sixth Synod, held in Guernsey in 1576, the Governors of both Bailiwicks were present. The Synod agreed that all Islanders would follow the same Calvinist form of discipline and divine service in their churches.

In the next century, the conflict for possession of the Channel Islands came from a most unexpected quarter. Certainly French raids were still feared. Charles I sent twelve hundred English soldiers to defend Guernsey. In Jersey both Gorey Castle and St Aubin's Fort were strengthened and Hermitage Rock fortified. But what was Admiral Blake's English fleet doing in St Ouen's Bay in 1651?

The war between King and Parliament had then been raging for nine years; Jersey was for the King; Guernsey was for Parliament, except for its Royalist Governor who held Castle Cornet for his King. In 1646 the Prince of Wales had fled the fighting in England for a three month stay in Elizabeth Castle. Then, when, on Cromwell's orders, his father had been executed, he had not only been proclaimed King in Jersey's market place, but had come again to Elizabeth Castle for a further six months respite before fleeing to France. So, on Cromwell's orders, Admiral Blake's parliamentary forces were in St Ouen's Bay to invade and occupy Jersey.

St Aubin's Fort was the first to surrender, then Gorey and Elizabeth Castles. Castle Cornet was finally the last royalist stronghold in the whole of the British Isles to surrender to Cromwell.

With the eventual restoration of the monarchy in 1660, Guernsey, which - except for its Governor - had so openly been against the King, feared it might lose its former liberties but it too was included in Charles II's charter re-affirming all the Islands' privileges. Jersey's courageous loyalty, though, was especially recognised for, shortly after his accession, Charles II presented the Island's Bailiff with a silver gilt mace to carry when attending the Royal Court, or the States assembly, which he still does to this day.

There were, incidentally, important changes to the position of both Bailiffs and the Church in the 17th century. To begin with, the Bailiff together with the Dean, Vicomte, Attorney General and Solicitor General in Jersey and their counterparts in Guernsey were to be direct Crown appointments. Also, in Court and the States Assembly, the Bailiffs in both Bailiwicks were to be given precedence over the Islands' Governors. As for the Islands' churches, in 1620 the Calvinist system of church government was brought to an end. In 1783, however, Methodism first reached the Islands and its strong appeal was confirmed four years later when John Wesley himself came to preach to the Islanders in both Jersey and Guernsey. So it was not unexpected when the first Methodist chapel was opened in 1790 in Jersey's King Street, nor that Methodism has had such a strong influence during the two centuries since Wesley's visit in both Islands.

During the 1700's there were also several changes instituted by either England's Parliament or the Crown, many of which added yet further to the Islands' independence. In 1717 an Act of Parliament gave Islanders the right to export to England, free of duty, both goods and merchandise, providing that they were of their own growth or manufacture. Later, when smuggling had become almost a way of life for many Islanders, an Order in Council established both a permanent service of customs officers and a registrar's office). The following year the first chamber of commerce in the British Isles was founded in Jersey. Even more important, a year later, was when the States of Jersey received Royal approval for the code of laws they had drawn up. This finally established the elected States Members, not the Royal Court, as the Island's Legislative Assembly.

Both England and the Islands, however, still needed to be on guard against a French invasion. So, in Jersey, the defences of Fort Henry and Prince William were built on Gorey Common - right opposite the Normandy coast. But it was not until eighteen years later that France backed the rebelling American colonies and declared war on England. This declaration immediately set in process the hurried building of so-called Martello towers for the Islands' defence; it also prompted seamen from the two Bailiwicks to rush to London to register as privateers, after which they could legally stop French boats and seize their cargo.

A French invasion - via St Ouen's Bay - was actually attempted in 1779 but when the captains of the fleet saw the number of Jersey cannon ranged against them, they refused to sail any closer to the beach and retreated back to St Malo. The result of this near invasion was a States Order for guard houses to be built at the Island's most vulnerable sections of coastline. There followed two years of peace and then came a most bizarre attack on Jersey that had a most unexpected conclusion.

Just after Christmas, in 1780, the adventurer, Baron de Rullecourt, decided to help the French war effort by capturing Jersey. With his 1,200 men he set sail from Normandy to conquer the 4,000 English and Jersey soldiers defending the Island. To his surprise, when he eventually arrived at La Rocque on the 6th of January, 1781, no one was on duty in the guard house - they were at home celebrating the New Year.

Incredibly, without meeting any resistance, de Rullecourt marched from La Rocque to St. Helier's market place. From there he ordered a meeting with the Lieutenant Governor, telling him to surrender, as he was surrounded by four thousand French soldiers, with more to come. Moses Corbet, the Lieutenant Governor, not only believed him and surrendered immediately, but ordered all his troops to do so too.

Fortunately for Jersey, an English Officer, Major Peirson, stationed at Westmount, refused to obey this order. He swooped down with his

The 'Battle of Jersey' and the death of Major Peirson

troops to attack the French invaders still secure in the market square, with a cannon defending every entrance. Just as victory was his, the brave Major was killed by a musket ball through the heart. But the Baron was killed too, just twelve hours after he had marched so victoriously into the centre of St Helier.

In the Royal Square, where the market once was, is a stone marking the place where this last French invasion of Jersey failed. Both leaders have their last resting places in the Town Church just to the west of the Square where they fought in the Battle of Jersey. But despite this victory, Seymour Tower was built to defend La Rocque, while Guernsey Islanders started to build Fort George in their defence.

The last English occupation of the Islands was in 1651 and lasted nine years; the last French occupation of part of Jersey was in 1781 and lasted one day. During the next century, when the Islands were busy with their building of new roads and their fishing industry and Jersey had started its successful ship building, there were also invasion threats from Napoleon. These prompted the building of more towers and forts - including Jersey's Fort Regent - plus barracks for the British garrisons stationed in the Islands. The British Government even bought land to build a guard house in Jersey's Royal Square. But, after the victories of Trafalgar and Waterloo, the French threat to Great Britain and the Islands abated, while during the First World War, apart from many Islanders enlisting in the British Forces, life went on much as it had always done.

It was, however, later in the twentieth century that there was a third and unexpected occupation of all the Islands by a powerful force against which Islanders were quite defenceless. In fact, in 1940, on Churchill's orders, the Islands had been demilitarised; all British Forces taken off and evacuation plans made for all those who - with the enemy already marching towards Normandy - wanted to escape. There was the threat of a German invasion.

The French influence is very apparent in the Islands

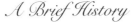

The German invasion of Guernsey was on 30th June 1940 and of Jersey on the next day. Then, after nearly five years of German troops - eventually numbering 35,000 - marching through their streets; taking their homes as billets; proclaiming new orders to obey; enforcing the use of German money and sticking Verboten notices around their beaches, Islanders then experienced an event both exciting and disappointing. In June 1944 they heard the roar of British planes flying over their Islands - it was D. Day, when British troops invaded German occupied Normandy. Once the allies had landed on French soil, Islanders imagined they would then free the Islands but the Allies' ultimate target was Berlin, not the Bailiwicks.

In fact, the Normandy landing brought the Islanders greater hardship then they had ever had to bear. No longer could the Germans, or the Islands' representatives, buy food and other items in France as they had during the past four years. By the autumn Islanders were near starvation, so Churchill was asked to lift the British blockade of the Islands so that food could be brought in. He refused, stating that the food would be taken by the Germans to prolong their resistance. Then, in November, the two Bailiffs applied to the Red Cross in Geneva. The Red Cross agreed to send the Islanders food in time for Christmas. However, it did not arrive and Islanders suffered their worst Christmas of the whole Occupation. 'The Vega' did arrive eventually in Guernsey on the 27th of December with food parcels from New Zealand and in Jersey on the 1st of January 1945, with food parcels packed in Canada.

The news everyone had been waiting for came five months later, when Islanders heard the voice of Churchill over the radio on 8th May declaring 'And our dear Channel Islanders are also to be freed today.' But it was the next day when the German Commander-in-Chief finally agreed to surrender and British troops, to the excited delight of the Islanders, stepped once more on Channel Island shores. They would never forget Liberation Day, 9th May 1945.

Sark, Alderney, Guernsey and Jersey are all self-governing islands, but they have all evolved quite differently from each other. Sark's Government or Chief Pleas is led by its Seigneur who appoints the Seneschal as the Court's President. Also attending its three meetings a year is the Prevot, Greffier, forty of the Seigneur's tenants (property owners) and twelve Deputies. Alderney too, though part of the Guernsey Bailiwick as well, has its own States Assembly, with an elected President and twelve States Members, plus a Clerk and a Treasurer. Both Guernsey and Jersey have Bailiffs who preside over their States Assemblies. In Guernsey Conseilleurs, Deputies and Parish Douzaine representatives and two States Members from Alderney sit in their States. In Jersey the States Members are either Senators, Parish Constables or Deputies. Present in both States Assemblies, and allowed to voice their opinions, are the Dean of each of the Bailiwick's and the Crown Officers appointed to it - such as Guernsey's H.M. Procureur and Jersey's Attorney General - but none of these may cast a vote.

The Monarch's representative in each Bailiwick, with a direct link to the Home Office, is the Lieutenant Governor. He may attend a States meeting, but may neither speak nor vote in it. The Home Office never interferes with the Islands' domestic affairs, as the Islands are not part of the United Kingdom. They are internally self governing dependencies of the Crown with - as we have seen - their own legal systems and courts. Neither are the Islands part of the E.U. as they negotiated their own special terms, which included trading but excluded E.U. membership. Britain's Parliament would, however, represent the Islands, if necessary, in foreign affairs, as they are part of the British Isles.

The Islands' different systems of government have worked well over the centuries, with law and order an especially high priority. They all prosper in their independence and still show evidence of the strong influence of both France and England which so affected their development.

Chapter Two

Manor Houses and Seigneurs

In the feudal times of the early 11th century after Normandy had taken over the civil and ecclesiastical administration of the Channel Islands, the Dukes of Normandy used the land on the Islands as gifts to reward the loyalty of - or to carry favour with - their most important subjects. These gifts of Island estates were known as 'fiefs' and varied considerably in size. So, to begin with, Guernsey was divided only into two fiefs of more or less equal size and these were given to the Norman Viscounts of Cotentin and Bessin. In Jersey, however, one of the first families to be granted a fief in the Island as well as having land in Normandy were the de Carterets, who were granted the fief of St Ouen on the Island's west coast.

In return for their Island fiefs, these Lords, or Seigneurs, of their estates would show their continued homage and loyalty to the Duke of Normandy by repaying him with their services or dues. So, for instance, if necessary, they would raise an army of men in their fief to protect him.

Local people already owning or living on land in a Seigneur's fief - mostly fishermen and farmers - became 'tenants' of their Seigneur. They, in their turn, repaid him for the privilege of living on his estate by agreeing to give him their service and a rent. So they were prepared to defend him

St Ouen's Manor, Jersey's oldest ancestral home

against his enemies; give him an annual amount of corn, fowls, pigs, flour and other produce; clean his colombier (dove-cot) and cart his loads of hay to his manor. These tenants, though, as they often owned their own freehold, could in no way be considered as serfs of their Seigneur.

By 1200 the larger fiefs had usually been sub-divided into smaller ones, many of which became the property of rich monasteries in Normandy. After the Channel Islands had become wholly under the jurisdiction of the English Crown in 1206, the non-ecclesiastical fiefs still existed however and the Seigneurs merely changed their allegiance to King John and his successors. They continued to protect the interests of their tenants through the courts they had set up in their fiefs where they administered the law and settled such matters as boundary disputes. They also often built mills in their fiefs where their tenants could grind their corn.

The senior Seigneurs also still kept their peculiar rights. These included the right to impound stray pigs and cattle; to keep wrecked ships and their contents washed up on the shores of their particular fief; and - once the Royal Court had found them guilty - to hang malefactors in their fief on their own gallows.

When it came to a Seigneur's individual service to his Sovereign when he visited the Channel Islands, the duty expected of him varied. In Jersey, for example, as their Sovereign's boat approached land, the Seigneurs of Rozel, Augrès and Samarès were expected to meet and greet him by riding in to the sea towards him until the water covered their spurs. Trinity's Seigneur had to present two mallards to the Monarch which, as recently as 1976, caused a problem as the then Seigneur, Major Riley explained; 'Ducks are always supposed to be reared in readiness for a Sovereign's visit on the manorial ponds. Unfortunately, though, on the Queen's visit my own ducks' plumage wasn't very colourful at that time of year, so I had to bag two off Gerald Durrell at Augrès Manor!"

As for Rozel's Seigneur, once he had dismounted from his horse, his orders were clearly set down for him to obey. 'As long as he (the King) tarry in the Isle, you shall act as his butler, and receive for your fee what the King's butler hath.'

In Guernsey the Sovereign pays for the dinner at the three sittings of the Court of Chief Pleas, the Island's high feudal court, which take place in January, at Easter and at Michaelmas. To these sittings all Guernsey's Seigneurs are obliged to come or to send an advocate to represent them in their absence. It is to this Court of Chief Pleas that all the Island's Seigneurs came to pay their homage to their Sovereign on Queen Elizabeth's recent visits to Guernsey.

It is interesting to note that, as Alderney is not divided into fiefs and has now no manor houses, there are, in fact, no Seigneurs on the Island. In 1042 William the Conqueror gave Alderney to the Monastery of Mont St. Michael - fifteen years later Alderney was given to the Bishop of Countances and most of the Island remained in that diocese for three centuries.

The title 'Lord of Alderney' was first used from about 1190, when the Crown gave the whole island to William L'Ingeniour. Subsequent titles given to Alderney's rules have included 'Lord of the Manor and of the People of the Island' - when John Chamberlain converted The Nunnery to his residence, having paid Elizabeth I twenty pounds for the Island's lease - and 'Governor of Alderney.' This last title was first adopted by Sir William Essex in about 1620, though no patent was ever given to him by the Crown to call himself that.

Today Alderney has no Governor and no Seigneurs but is managed by all twelve members of its States. They have been praised as 'The elected representatives of a self-governing people sitting in deliberative assemblies in which there were neither political parties or even "Government" and "Opposition" but all bent on deciding every question on its merits, and at the same time serving gratis. However, as the States of Guernsey are responsible for Alderney's finances, all their project expenses and budget proposals must be presented to Guernsey for their States' approval.

As we have already seen how Sark's most famous Dame, Sybil Hathaway, governed her fief, together with her husband - the Island's Seigneur - let us now turn our attention to the two Islands who did and still do have Seigneurs and let us focus on two famous families, one from Guernsey and one from Jersey, who have paid a major seigneural part in their Island's history.

It is thought that William de Salinelles, also known as William de Saumareis, was born at the end of the twelfth century. It is not known, though, when exactly this Jersey Seigneur of Samares, a fief in St Clement, was granted a fief in the Guernsey parish of St Martins and called the manor he built there Samares too. But his manor in Guernsey is spelt 'Sausmarez,' as is the name of his descendants, to this day. Except for a gap of two hundred years when, in Tudor times, John Andros became Seigneur, inheriting the title from his mother Judith de Sausmarez who had married the Englishman John Andrews, or Andros, the original de Sausmarez family have remained Seigneurs of the fief. In fact, as early as 1331 the fief is mentioned as having belonged to William's grandson Matthew 'from time immemorial.'

And how William and Matthew's descendants have added to the reputation of Guernsey through the centuries in so many different ways! In the eighteenth century six boys were born into the Sausmarez family whose names are still remembered with pride. There was Captain Philip de Sausmarez who not only proved himself an intrepid seaman on board H.M.S. Centurion in the war against Spain, but also, in four years, circumnavigated the globe; seized treasure worth £600,000, enabling the Fief de Sausmarez to be bought back from the Andros family; and designed the uniform adopted by Royal Navy Officers in the reign of

George II. A memorial to his achievements can still be seen in the north aisle of the choir in Westminster Abbey.

Philip de Sausmarez's younger brother Thomas found fame during the seven years war against France. In 1758, when Thomas was stationed in Bristol, he heard that the French ship 'Belliqueux,' with sixty-four guns ready to fire at the enemy, was anchored off Ilfracombe. The warship had, apparently, lost its top foremost and was short of both water and food. So, despite a strong head wind, Thomas got aboard H.M.S. Antelope, which was then under his command, and sailed her along the coast to Ilfracombe. He and his crew captured the Belliqueux on 2nd November 1758. When he returned to Bristol with his prize, it was added to the Royal Navy and Thomas became its captain.

Another Thomas de Sausmarez did not follow the naval tradition started by Philip and his brother. This Thomas had a distinguished career as a Guernsey lawyer. At eighteen he became Comptroller de Sa Majesté, or Solicitor General; in 1795 he succeeded to the office of Procureur, or Attorney General. In all Thomas served his Island as Law Officer of the Crown for fifty-six years. He also fathered twenty-eight children - twelve by his first wife, Martha and sixteen by his second, Catherine - and became Seigneur in 1820.

Before the German Occupation of Guernsey there used to be an obelisk in Delancey Park, originally erected to honour the memory of yet another 18th century de Sausmarez. This was James, First Baron de Sausmarez of Guernsey, G.C.B, K.B, D.C.L, Admiral of the Red and General of Marines. He is still acknowledged as the Island's greatest naval hero and his most famous exploits were in the French Revolutionary War which started in 1793 and the Napoleonic Wars, which followed. He started off in 1793, when, as Captain of H.M.S. Crescent, he managed to capture, despite its thirty-six guns, the French frigate 'La Réunion' just off Cherbourg. It was for this brave action that he was knighted.

James also distinguished himself at Cape Vincent against Napoleon in 1797 and became Nelson's second-in-command at the Battle of the Nile the following year. His next victory, for which he was created a Knight of the Bath, was against the Spanish and French off Gibraltar in July 1801. This was such a magnificent victory for the Royal Navy that James was also given the Freedom of the City of London, awarded with a handsome pension of £1,200 and had Nelson himself give him a vote of thanks for his brave service in the House of Lords.

As if all that were not enough to establish his reputation, James was next put in charge of a naval squadron to patrol the Baltic. He managed to contain the French forces and keep them from action against Sweden for five years, until Napoleon's devastating defeat in 1812. His memory is still honoured in Sweden to this day.

General Sir Thomas Saumarez also saw action in the French Revolutionary War but not in the same way as his brother James, Thomas was given the important post of Brigade-Major of the Guernsey Militia. Just across the water were the French, anxious to stop Guernsey privateers looting and seizing French boats. So a keen eye had to be kept on their activities. Not only was Thomas responsible for the surveillance of French emigrés who had come to Guernsey to escape the war but he also had to recruit from among them secret agents who could return to mainland France and then bring back important information.

Thomas was so highly thought of that, in 1795, the States of Guernsey asked him to represent the Island by carrying a Loyal Address to London on the occasion of the wedding of the Prince of Wales. George III then knighted him.

In 1812, when the American War of Independence started, Thomas was given command of the Halifax garrison in Nova Scotia. A year later he was also acting as New Brunswick's Commander-in-Chief. But, once the war was over, Thomas became Groom of the Bedchamber to Victoria's father, the Duke of Kent, and on Queen Victoria's coronation in 1938 Thomas was promoted to the position of General, his final honour. He died, back in Guernsey, at the age of eighty-five.

The younger brother of James and Thomas, Dr. Richard Sausmarez, when still in his teens left Guernsey to become a medical student at the London Hospital and, in 1785, a Member of the Surgeon's company. Though his wife Martha was also a Channel Islander - she was the daughter of Alderney's Governor at that time - he never returned to live in Guernsey. He became a surgeon in Newington Butts in 1786 and, two years later, was appointed surgeon at Streatham's Magdalene Hospital. On his resignation from this post, in 1805, Richard took up private practice and became well known for his books and papers on medical matters which put forward ideas which were ahead of their time.

Richard retired to Bath and died there in 1835. A memorial tablet to Richard and his family was later taken from Newington Butts and placed in Bath Abbey where it can still be seen. A fine tribute to the youngest of the de Sausmarez family born in the 18th century to find fame beyond the shores of Guernsey.

And the Seigneurs in the Sausmarez family in the twentieth century? After a distinguished career as a judge in the Colonial Service, Sir Havilland de Sausmarez was back in Guernsey just in time for the Royal visit there in 1921. As Seigneur of the Sausmarez fief and therefore hereditary Third Butler to his Sovereign, Sir Havilland acted as cupbearer to King George V and Queen Mary. All this job entailed in the twentieth century, in fact, was to serve tea to his Royal visitors!

A year later Sir Havilland was appointed Guernsey's Bailiff. In that capacity and with the eventual co-operation of Jersey's Bailiff, he fought a fierce battle with the British Government which lasted until 1927. The British Government was demanding a large annual contribution from the two Bailiwicks towards the cost of Imperial Defence. The two Bailiffs - following Sir Havilland's suggestion - were offering a 'once-for-all-gift.'

This is what the British Government was finally obliged to accept.

When German forces occupied Guernsey in July 1940, Sir Havilland had retired from the position of Bailiff, but he had not lost his sense of humour. When the Germans gave the order that all boats had to be taken to St Peter Port Harbour by the 1st of October, 1940, Sir Havilland had a question for them. Did the order include the punt, which he used at Sausmarez Manor to trim the banks of the Manor's pond?

Cecil de Sausmarez was the Seigneur who sponsored, with Jersey's Senator Dupré, the Official History of the Occupation Years. The two Presidents of their Island's States chose Dr Charles Cruickshank to write the book and it was published under the auspices of the Trustees of the Imperial War Museum in 1975.

Cecil, however, was not born in Guernsey. He was born in Rawalpindi where his Captain father was serving. He was educated in England and taught there until January 1939 when he was appointed Attaché to the British Embassy in Brussels. When the Germans swept into Belgium in May 1940 he made his escape, via Dunkirk, back to London.

For the rest of the war Cecil served first at the Ministry of Information and then at the Political Warfare Executive. In both posts he had special responsibility for the Low Countries. Once Belgium had been liberated, however, Cecil immediately returned to the Brussels Embassy as First Secretary. He was subsequently awarded the MBE in recognition of his valuable contribution to the war effort.

In 1947, on the death of the Dame of Sausmarez - Sir Havilland's widow - Cecil became, in accordance with his uncle's wishes, the next Seigneur. To live in Sausmarez Manor was not, though, a new experience for him. He had spent some part of every summer holiday there - except, of course, during the years of Guernsey's Occupation - all his life.

After continuing to work part of the year in England for several years, Cecil finally returned to Guernsey for good on 1st January 1959. Not only did he then serve his Island as its premier Seigneur, paying homage to Queen Elizabeth in 1957 and 1978 on behalf of all Guernsey's Seigneurs, but from 1961 to 1979, he was the elected Deputy for the parish of St Martins. Cecil also became President of both the States of Guernsey History 1939 - 45 Committee and La Société Guernsiaise.

The present Seigneur of Sausmarez is Peter de Sausmarez. He and his family are faced with the task of both maintaining and restoring the manor house, which suffered damage in the floods and hurricane of 1987. The expense of the work that now has to be carried out is partly met by opening the house and grounds to visitors and by allowing both to be used for such occasions as weddings, receptions, seminars, conferences and balls. The present Seigneur is also much encouraged by the restoration of the manor's unique and rare tapestries being undertaken by an Island charitable trust.

To visit Sausmarez Manor - which as well as being a home is also a historic landmark of Guernsey's history, stretching back for nearly a thousand years - is also a way of paying tribute to the remarkable Sausmarez family which has enhanced Guernsey's reputation so well for so long.

Just as Guernsey's first family came originally from elsewhere - Jersey, in fact - so Jersey's first family, the de Carterets, came originally from Carteret - a small town almost opposite Jersey on the Cotentin coast. So, as well as being Seigneurs of the fief of St. Ouen, they also had much larger estates where they were Lords of the Manor in Normandy.

When, however, in 1204 King John of England lost Normandy which, since the time of William the Conqueror, had been ruled in conjunction with England, the de Carterets had to make a choice. Would they swear allegiance to the King of France or the King of England? They chose to remain loyal to King John but, as a result, lost all their property in Normandy.

Like the de Sausmarez family, the de Carterets also decided sometimes to shorten their surname. So Sir George de Carteret - Jersey's Bailiff and Lieutenant Governor, as well as Treasurer of the Royal Navy - was granted land in America by a grateful Charles II in the name of George Carteret, just as several of the de Sausmarez family found fame under the abbreviated name of Saumarez.

During the many centuries the de Carterets were Jersey's leading family, they provided nine Lieutenant Governors, fifteen Bailiffs, nine Attorney-Generals and nearly fifty Jurats to maintain law and order in their Island. They also had two special traditions to distinguish the part they played in Island life. If a de Carteret was appointed Jurat, he claimed the right to sit next to the Bailiff in the Royal Court. Then, when a Governor of Jersey died in office, the Seigneur of St Ouen took it upon himself to command the troops in the Island until a new Governor was appointed.

Their good offices, though, were also highly thought of and appreciated by English monarchs. Elizabeth I granted Sark to the de Carterets 'in reward of the many services received by herself and her royal ancestors from this family.' Nearly a hundred years later Charles II granted Alderney to the de Carterets in gratitude for their taking the Royalist side in the Civil War.

Being Seigneurs of all they surveyed, however, did not necessarily ensure that their lives would be ones of leisure, pleasure and plenty. They could be sent by their Sovereign on dangerous exploits; they could face a revolt of their tenants; they could be wrongfully sentenced to death. Following the lives of just one de Carteret from each century from the 18th back to the 14th shows just how full of adventure and danger a Seigneur's life could be.

Jersey fiefs held at various times by the de Carterets included Longueville, Rozel, Avranches, Vinchelez de Bas and Trinity. Philip de Carteret, Captain in the Royal Navy, inherited Trinity Manor on the death of his father in 1796. Between becoming Trinity's Seigneur and his most daring naval exploit fifteen years later, he proved his loyalty to his Sovereign by capturing the Dutch schooner 'L'Honneur,' complete with a cargo of arms on board for the Dutch fleet; in 1806 and 1807 he captured a French ship - which meant two less enemy ships to attack the British fleet.

It was in 1811, though, that Philip had his finest hour as a British Naval Commander. He was in command of the 46-gun frigate 'Naiad' as it was approaching the north coast of France. Napoleon just happened then to be holding a naval review at Boulogne. When the Naiad suddenly sailed into Napoleon's view, his immediate order was for twelve gun praams (a praam being flat bottomed boat with guns), ten brigs and a sloop to sail out to her and capture her.

For two and a half hours Philip fought the flotilla of French boats until, as night began to fall, they were forced to take shelter near their shore batteries' defence. During the night three brigs and a cutter came to reinforce the Naiad's position off Boulogne. But the French had reinforcements too. When the sun rose no fewer than twenty-two ships sailed forth to attack the five British boats.

Philip's order was for his five boats to sail right into the midst of the French squadron. They were not, however, to fire any of their guns until they were within pistol-shot range of the enemy. Philip himself was just about to board and capture the French Admiral's praam when the 'Ville de Lyons' suddenly sailed between it and the Naiad. His reaction was straight away to lash his boat to the side of the Ville de Lyons. In Philip's own words: 'The small arms men soon cleared her deck, and the boarders, sword in hand, completed her subjugation.' The French were, therefore, forced yet again to retire towards their shore defences. De

Carteret, meanwhile, set about sailing his captured French prize back to England.

Despite all his naval engagements, Philip never forgot his responsibilities as Seigneur of Trinity. After his retirement in 1817 he spent most of his time back in this Manor and, after his death in 1828, a local paper called the 'Chronique' said of him: 'The poor feel that they have lost a friend and a protector, and the parishioners of Trinity do not tire of praising all the good he has done.'

The story of one of the de Carterets born in the 17th century was quite different. For one thing, Charles - the only son of the 8th Sir Philippe de Carteret and Elizabeth, daughter of Trinity's Sir Edouard de Carteret - was Seigneur of the family's original Jersey fief of St Ouen. Knighted when he was only 8 and taking over his late father's position of Bailiff when he came of age, Charles was suddenly confronted in 1701 by the unexpected. His tenants were in revolt against him. The chiefs, or heads, of his fief's cinquantaines, or divisions, took him to court. They wanted to know 'by what right he claimed annually from each cinquaintaine a cart load of vraic (seaweed), the digging of a vergée of land, the cartage of wood and stone for the repair of the manor buildings and manual labour.'

And what a can of worms that Court case was to open! First the Court ordered a Commission, made up of six men from each of the two sides in dispute, to draw up a report on the services that were actually due from the tenants to the Seigneur. The tenants, once they had seen the list of duties expected from them - which included providing an escort to take prisoners from St Ouen's to the prison in St Helier, from the prison to the Court and from thence, if guilty, back to the Seigneur's own gallows in St Ouen - appealed to the Privy Council in England. Not only did the tenants' appeal fail but they were ordered to pay the costs of the inquiry.

Then came two more Court cases. Jean Tourgis, Greffier of the Seigneurial Court, who should have known better where his true allegiance lay, was prosecuted for giving the tenants a copy of an important paper that belonged to St Ouen's Manor.   Next, it was the turn of the tenants' leader, Simon de Caen.   He was found guilty of suggesting that Charles de Carteret had ordered Tourgis 'to endeavour to recover the paper by subtlety or violence.' Both men were found guilty, fined and ordered to ask for pardon from their Seigneur on their knees.

When Sir Charles de Carteret died in 1715, his demise brought to an end the direct male line of the de Carterets who had inherited the St Ouen fief, son from father, for nearly seven hundred years.

In the 16th century, far from antagonising his tenants, Helier de Carteret, when he took over the Fief of St. Ouen in 1552, gave a banquet for over two hundred guests which included them too. Helier was also quick to realise the danger to Jersey, but especially to St Ouen's parish if the then deserted island of Sark should be taken over by either the French or marauding pirates.

So, in 1563, Helier sailed over to Guernsey and spoke of his concern both to the Island's Governor and the Royal Commissioners who happened to be in Guernsey at that time. They, in turn, told Queen Elizabeth of the possible danger to the Islands and, in 1565, Helier received letters patent from her. This outlined both the result of an uninhabited Sark - the Queen had lost her revenue and the Island's creeks had become pirates' lairs - and the remedy - to fill the Island with the Queen's subjects. The Queen, therefore, gave Sark to Helier and his heirs in return for an annual payment of fifty shillings. Helier could hold a Court there, establish markets and put a tax on beer, wine and bread. A final condition was that Sark was, from then on, to be inhabited by at least forty men living there permanently.

Helier's first move that same year was to sail to Sark with his wife and some of his servants. All they found to live in was a ruined chapel. So they immediately had to clear some land of all the rabbit holes, brambles, bracken and undergrowth, with which most of the Island was covered to build themselves houses. Helier then had brought over from Jersey, and man-handled up the cliffs, all the building materials they would need, farm implements, corn and vegetable seeds, horses, cattle and pigs. In the end, Helier had a settlement of forty houses, each complete with its own garden.

Helier, though, still paid attention to his duties in St Ouen as Seigneur, to Jersey as its senior Jurat and as leader of the newly formed Puritan Party. In Mary's reign he refused to go to the Catholic mass and, instead, had sailed to Normandy to receive communion at the Huguenot church in St. Lô. In Elizabeth's reign he had the Privy Council's permission to use the Huguenot service book in the Town Church of both St Peter Port and St Helier. Helier had, in fact, accomplished a great deal in many different aspects of Channel Island life by the time of his death in 1581. The last two representatives of the de Carteret family were both wrongfully sentenced to death but for quite different reasons. In 1470 when Philippe de Carteret, the heir to St Ouen's Fief, was fourteen, a marriage was arranged between him and Margaret Harliston, the sixteen year old daughter of Jersey's first Governor, Sir Richard Harliston. Little did either of them realise at that stage what an important part Margaret was eventually to play in Phillipe's life.

Political matters were to divide Jerseymen during the Civil War between the Yorkists and the Lancastrians and their followers in Jersey. In addition, an Englishman in the Island caused his own complications. That fact, too, played an important part in Philippe's life. After the Lancastrian Henry Tudor had defeated the Yorkist Richard III, the new King appointed Matthew Baker and another friend of his (who spent most of his time in England) as Governors of Jersey. In reality, Matthew Baker became Jersey's second Governor but, being an Englishman, he knew nothing about Jersey life, its traditions or its customs and, unlike his predecessor, Sir Richard Haliston, was not concerned to learn about them.

One of the first things that Matthew Baker did was to ask all the Island's Seigneurs to produce their title deeds to prove the legitimacy of their Seigneural claims. Not only that, he then immediately increased the rent on all Crown lands. Understandably the Seigneurs were appalled by both these demands of Matthew Baker. Philippe de Carteret, as he was by then Jersey's senior Seigneur, agreed to protest to the Privy Council in England against Baker's high handedness.

Baker was furious at Philippe's action and there and then determined to get rid of him. First of all Baker forged a letter addressed to some noblemen in Normandy, offering to give Mont Orgueil up to the French, so that they could once more rule Jersey. Baker signed the letter with Philippe's name, had it dropped by one of his men in a lane near Longueville Manor and then pretended to find it as he rode down the lane on his way to St Helier.

Once in St Helier, Baker took the letter straight to the Royal Court and threw the letter down in front of the Bailiff, as Philippe, who was in Court as a Jurat, watched. Baker then accused Philippe of being a traitor in front of the Bailiff and his fellow Jurats. Philippe was horrified by the charge and naturally straight away denied that he had written the letter.

Baker, though, had expected this denial and told the Bailiff that the only way to determine the truth was by the ancient and, by then, the almost obsolete Ordeal by Battle. He also chose his henchman, Le Boutillier, as the one to fight Philippe in this club duel to decide which man was telling the truth. The Bailiff agreed to Baker's plan, committed both men to be imprisoned in Mont Orgueil until the day of the Ordeal by Battle, fixed for St Lawrence's Day, on the 10th of August 1494. Once they were inside the Castle, Baker ordered that his champion, Le Boutillier, be fed like a fighting cock and allowed to walk about the Castle in the fresh air.

Philippe, on the other hand, was to be kept in his damp, dark cell and fed on bread and water. Baker's final order was that no one should leave Jersey. He had no wish for one of Philippe's friends to sail to England and tell Henry VII what he had done.

At this point Margaret, Philippe's wife, heard of her husband's dire predicament. Despite having given birth to one of their children just three days before, she determined to do something to save his life. First she found a fisherman from St Ouen to take her secretly to Guernsey; from there she found someone to take her to England in his sloop. Once in England, she sought an audience with King Henry. He at once wrote an Order forbidding the Ordeal by Battle. He also arranged that the charge of treason against her husband should be judged in England by the Privy Council.

Margaret's next move was to return to Jersey as soon as possible before the day of the Battle. Fortunately, she found a boat bound for Jersey at Southampton and arrived back in the Island just in time - on St. Lawrence's Eve. When the Bailiff was shown the King's Order, he had no option but to stop the Ordeal by Battle. And when Philippe was eventually tried for treason by the Privy Council he was found innocent and Matthew Baker was relieved of his position as Governor of Jersey.

In 1356, during the Hundred Years War with France, Sir Renaud de Carteret, the Seigneur of St Ouen was sentenced to death for quite a different reason. When the French captured Cornet Castle yet again that year, Sir Renaud, along with the Seigneurs of Trinity and St Germain and other Jerseymen, 'assembled their strength, and after a severe combat took the Captain of the Castle, who ransomed himself from there for 80,000 florins.' A prominent Guernseyman, William Le Feyure, was then 'slain as a traitor and adherent of the enemy by the common consent of the armed men and others there present.'

This summary execution caused deep resentment in Guernsey.

Sausmarez Manor, Guernsey

William's wife, the sister of the Seigneur of Sausmarez, at once had all those who caused her husband's execution arrested and had them charged at Guernsey's Court with murder. Renaud, who had been at neither the court-martial of William, nor at his execution, nevertheless told Guernsey's Bailiff that 'the accused had nothing to be ashamed of' and that in that case 'he was as blameworthy as any of those impeached.'

On hearing this, the Bailiff and his Jurats found Renaud guilty and had him imprisoned. n 1357 the King himself gave an Order to have the prisoners released, as it had been "testified before the Council that William was a traitor at the time of his death". This Order incensed William's wife and she pleaded to the King for a new Order, showing that 'William, at the time he was slain, was under the King's special protection as liegeman and that he was killed out of ancient enmity and malice and not for treason.'

Renaud was then re-arrested and once more imprisoned in Castle Cornet, the same castle that he had made such a valiant effort to recapture from the French. The King, however, had not forgotten his valour and, in March 1359, sent a letter patent which stated that 'because he was not at the killing or consenting to it "the King" has pardoned him, whatever the Bailiff or Jurats have recorded against him.' Sir Renaud died in 1382, while the Frenchman, Admiral de Vienne, was occupying - but fortunately not devastating - both Jersey and Guernsey, under the terms of the Treaty of Paris, drawn up by France and Castile.

It was certainly an honour to be a Seigneur in either Guernsey or Jersey and there was certainly plenty of land to survey in the large fiefs of Sausmarez and St. Ouen. Life, however, in such an exalted position definitely had its own responsibilities, with public service a priority. Sometimes there were also brave deeds to be done in the name of one's Sovereign and sometimes there was even the treat of lawful execution to be faced by Seigneurs quite innocent of any wrong doing.

One of the stained glass windows inside St Ouen's Manor depicts the historical background of the Malet de Carteret family

Some manors have been converted into luxury hotels or tourist attractions.
Above: Longeuville Manor, Jersey. Below: Samares Manor, Jersey

**La Seigneurie Manor and Gardens, feudal home of the
Seigneur of Sark**

Mr Malet de Carteret of St Ouen may be the present Seigneur of all he surveys round his fine manor house - thoughtfully fortified against the French by his ancestor, Philippe, with the permission of Jersey's first Governor, Sir Richard Harliston - but, let us hope he is not faced by any of the more dreaded events endured by his forefathers.

What Mr. Malet de Carteret can look forward to, though, is renewed interest in the de Carteret family tree. Why? The Spencer family, represented today by Earl Spencer, brother of the late Princess Diana, are direct descendants of the de Carterets. It happened in the time of George II when Lord John Carteret's daughter, Lady Georgina Carteret, married the Honourable John Spencer of Althorp. Their son became the first Earl Spencer. And to prove this unexpected connection with the Royal Princes, William and Harry, there is a window in St Ouen's Manor bearing a coat of arms with the family's name clearly there for all to see - 'Spencer.'

Chapter Three

Famous Visitors and Residents From the Past

It is not at all surprising that, because of their extensive and appealing seascapes together with their inland tranquillity, the Islands have always enticed visitors to their shores. Some of these visitors have only spent a short time here, such as the French writer and diplomat Chateaubriand, who came to Jersey for four months to be with his uncle, a refugee from the terrors of the French Revolution. Others, like Billy Butlin (Jersey) of Holiday Camp fame; T.H. White (Alderney) who wrote 'Sword in the Stone,' the television food presenter Fanny Craddock (Guernsey) and Sir Compton Mackenzie (Herm and Jethou) author of the comic 'Whisky Galore' actually spent many years living in their favoured island.

What is surprising, though, is the larger number of Islanders - considering the Islands' small population - who have made a name for themselves beyond their own shores. From Alderney there is the surgeon Sir Henry Gauvain who, in 1920, was knighted for his services to crippled children and, in 1936, was awarded the Distinguished Service Gold Key of the American Congress of Physical Therapy. From Guernsey, as well as the actor Roy Dotrice, there is the Island's greatest 18th century soldier, Major General Sir Isaac Brock who has, in honour of his valour, Ontario's Brock University named after him as well as a

One of France's most celebrated writers, Victor Hugo, spent a period of his life in both Jersey and Guernsey

monument in St Paul's Cathedral. Also from Guernsey is the great 19th century entrepreneur Thomas de la Rue who founded the London house of de la Rue and Sons which still prints banknotes and stamps for the British Isles.

Worldwide fame has come to several Jerseymen too. In the 18th century there is Philippe de Carteret, the circumnavigator, who it is said ranked 'among the greatest geographical discoverers of his time.' In the same century, as well as the marine painter, Peter Monamy, there was also the poet and schoolmaster Richard Valpy who, in 1781, became head of Reading Grammar School and during the fifty-five years he was there made it one of England's finest schools. Later there was the painter John Millais and the golfer Harry Varden to bring publicity to the Island where they first learned their skills and showed their talents.

Now let us look more closely at some famous visitors and renowned Islanders, past and present, who brought special fame to the Islands of their birth.

VICTOR HUGO

The first visitor lived for some time in both Jersey and Guernsey, but had quite a different reputation in each Island. He was the 19th century French writer Victor Hugo, the author of 'Les Miserables.'

'Ravissant' was the adjective our most illustrious visitor applied to Jersey when he fled here, seeking refuge in order to escape Louis Napoleon's anger. He was less flattering, though, when asked to leave the island three years later.

A staunch republican, Hugo, with dismay, had seen his countrymen first vote Louis Napoleon President and then, in December 1852, proclaim him Emperor. The distrust was mutual, for the new Napoleon III lost no time in expelling Hugo, together with sixty-seven other republican deputies.

Belgium was Hugo's first refuge, but the government there became uneasy, harbouring a pamphleteer who spent his time vilifying 'Little Napoleon.' So Hugo was forced to seek asylum elsewhere and chose Jersey.

His arrival in St Helier caused a great stir, for at that time there were many political refugees from various countries in Jersey, and they all trooped down to the quay to greet him. Never at a loss for words, Hugo assured them that he had come to share the same sky, the same exile and that they were all to love one another.

He then went in triumph to La Pomme D'Or, where he stayed until he was lucky enough to find a pretty little house by the sea, 3 Marina Terrace, Grève d'Azette. There he stayed with his wife, children and sons-in-law, a self-contained group of six, for three years. His mistress, Juliette Drouet, was conveniently found lodgings just along the coast at Havre de Pas. The Hugo's did not mix much with the local people, but had family picnics at St. Brelade, enjoyed the sea views and the younger ones loved to have steeple chases on the beach.

The comparative uneventfulness of this life enabled Hugo to return to his poetry and, while in Jersey, he wrote both 'Les Châtiments' and most of 'Les Contemplations.' One Jersey poem, written at Grève d'Azette, records that though he had been nipped by a crab, he had been generous enough to throw the creature back into the sea!

However, as he pointed out in the many letters he wrote to his friends, he could not be for ever writing or admiring the scenery - more stimulating diversions were demanded. The most harmless of these, and one in keeping with his artistic temperament, was the newly discovered art of photography.

His son Charles managed to acquire all the equipment from the continent, so the great man was posed against the most gothic of Jersey scenery, such as bare rocks, or the interior of a grotto. The skillful contrast of shade and light in the photos emphasised that here was an Olympian, questioning both God and Destiny..

Of a slightly more dubious nature were the diversions of table-turning and playing billiards on a Sunday. This last was done behind closed shutters so as not to shock the natives!

The liveliest activity, which was to prove his downfall, was Hugo's continued support of Republican ideas and he seized every opportunity to spread these 'Red' sentiments. He delivered the funeral oration at Macpéla cemetery at the death of every exile; he spoke on the anniversaries of the Polish revolution as well as on the Proclamation of France's Second Republic. The villain in all these orations was, of course, Napoleon III.

He was also a supporter of the exiles' Jersey newspaper 'L'Homme' which had had the temerity in October to reprint a scurrilous letter written to Queen Victoria by a Republican fanatic, accusing her of unimaginable goings on in Paris during her return visit to Napoleon III. For this act of treason the editor, owner and distributor were all expelled from Jersey.

Hugo thought this expulsion without a trial to be outrageous and wrote a declaration saying so, which he had posted up in the streets of St Helier. Hugo's name topped the list of signatories and the Declaration concluded with the bravado 'Expel us too,' so, as Victor Hugo set sail for a new asylum in Guernsey, he looked back on Jersey no longer as beautiful and charming but as a mere 'nothing,'

There was a good omen, though, as Hugo, Juliette Drouet and his son sailed in the steamer to Guernsey because, as his son pointed out, 'We saw above it in the sky the column of smoke which was going to guide us towards another promised land.' As they came into St Peter Port there was already a crowd on the quay - silent but sympathetic - and the men took their hats off as the great man passed. Hugo's wife and the rest of his family followed him to Guernsey a few days later.

While they were looking for somewhere permanent to live, the family stayed at L'Hotel de L'Europe. Eventually the area known as Hauteville was discovered. Here they first of all rented Number 20, with Juliette in Number 44 and then, in 1856, Hugo bought Hauteville House for his family and Number 20 for Juliette, from where she could see his signals to her more clearly and where she received his two letters to her every day. Guests at Hauteville House were, apparently, introduced to Hugo's wife as 'Madame, the mother of my children' and to Juliette as 'Madame, my friend.'

Hauteville House with its peaceful garden was the perfect refuge for this French exile. Not only did its spacious rooms afford him the opportunity to try out his woodwork skills on their panels but also the chance to fill them with the furniture, tapestries, paintings, statues and porcelain that he loved to collect. The house also had the perfect room in which he could write. This was a small, sparsely furnished, glass walled study at the top of the house with a fine sea view and the silhouette of the coastline of his native France. At the two desks in there where he stood to write between 1862 and 1869, Hugo finished three novels: 'Les Miserables,' 'Les Travailleurs de la Mer' - based on his experience of living in Guernsey - and 'L'Homme Qui Ret.'

The Hugos, as in Jersey, did not mix much with the Islanders, despite their being French speaking, but a few who had interests in common with Hugo were invited to Hauteville House. One of them was Georges Métivier and Hugo was much stimulated by helping the Guernseyman to get his Franco-Norman dictionary ready for publication. When not working or playing the part of host - especially to fellow Republicans and exiles - Hugo and his family, just like many twentieth century Guernsey tourists, enjoyed boat trips to Sark - 'Le plus vieux poème en pierre qui surgese de la surface des eaux' and staying in The Dixart Hotel.

The Hugos lived happily in the tiny portion of France they had established in Guernsey for fifteen years. Then, in 1870 came news of the fall of Napoleon III. Victor Hugo, his family and his mistress returned as soon as they could to his beloved France. Their eccentric neighbour was not much missed by most Islanders, but the poor children in his neighbourhood must surely have felt his loss because, in the last seven years of his stay in Hauteville House, every Thursday without fail he had seen to it that they were served a good square meal.

When one goes to Candie Gardens to admire the statue of Hugo which commemorates his fifteen years exile in Guernsey, it seems a trifle ironic that he shares the Gardens with a statue of Queen Victoria. It was, after all, his upholding a fanatical Republican's criticism of the English Queen that led to his expulsion from Jersey, which, in its turn, led to his final exile in Guernsey.

LILLIE LANGTRY

Most people remember Lillie Langtry for being the mistress of Edward VII. What most people do not realise is that not only was she born outside the United Kingdom but that she also achieved much more in her long life.

Lillie was, in fact, born in 1853 in Jersey. She was the only daughter of the Rector of St Saviour and the Dean of Jersey, the Very Reverend William Corbet Le Breton. She was baptised in her father's church as Emilie Charlotte but in the family she was always called Lillie.

Having five older brothers and one of them, her favourite Reginald, two years younger had a great influence on Lillie's childhood. For one thing she joined in her brothers' games, such as haunting St Saviour's churchyard and stealing door knockers for trophies from nearby neighbours. She also enjoyed their same leisure pursuits, such as riding which led to one Jerseyman writing in his diary that it was 'imprudent to allow a girl of thirteen to ride a racer with a snaffle.'

No wonder she herself later commented that: 'Living the life of my brothers transformed me into an incorrigible tomboy.'

There was, however, a further, greater advantage to having six brothers - she shared in their education. Lillie's father insisted that when the boys' tutor came to the deanery every evening to supervise the homework set them by Victoria College, their sister should also be there to be taught Latin, Greek and Maths. She was also given lessons by masters specialising in French, German, drawing and music. No wonder therefore - with an education so unusual for a girl at that time - that when she was grown-up, men of the world such as Gladstone, Oscar Wilde and Bernard Shaw found her such a stimulating conversationalist as well as radiantly beautiful.

How, though, did a Jersey girl, even if she was the Dean's daughter, come to meet such important people? It all started when her brother William got married in his father's church; he asked his twenty year old sister to be a bridesmaid and one Edward Langtry, who had recently lost his wife, to be his best man. After the wedding ceremony, Edward gave a ball in honour of William and his bride at the Jersey Yacht Club. Lillie recalled the excitement of being there in her autobiography that 'it was a far more elaborate and extravagant affair than anything I had hitherto witnessed and it electrified me.'

But that was not the only entertainment Edward provided for his new Jersey friends. With the Dean as chaperone, he took Lillie on sailing trips in his yacht 'Red Gauntlet.' It is not surprising, therefore, that despite, or perhaps because of her parents opposition, Lillie accepted Edward's proposal of marriage and before long they were both in London, with Lillie longing to become part of its high society.

An introduction to London society, however, did not come immediately and, when it did, it came through an unexpected meeting. It came about through meeting a fellow Islander, John Millais, at a party where he

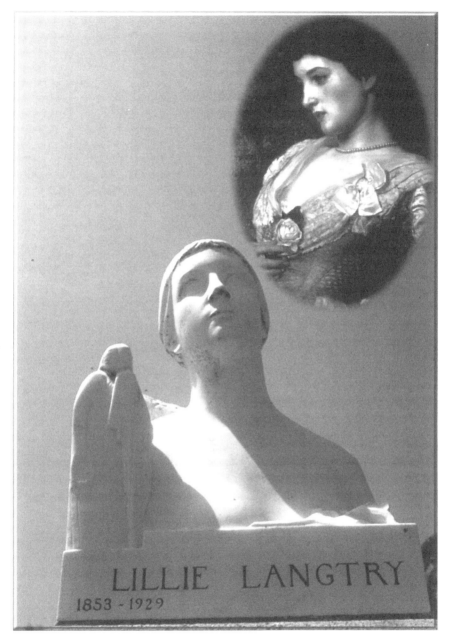

Lillie Langtry mixed in royal circles and later toured the United States where she also became a celebrity

Lillie's luxurious travel case can be found displayed in the Jersey Museum

'beamed a friendly enthusiasm while he claimed me as his country woman.' He also took her down to supper and not only delighted in speaking to her in Jersey Norman-French, but also asked whether she would sit for him. He said that he wanted to be the first painter of the 'classic features' of his countrywoman. The Millais painting of 'A Jersey Lily' immediately enhanced the reputation of Lillie's beauty, especially when it was hung in the Royal Academy and nominated in 1879 as picture of the year.

The very next day after this party - where Lillie was introduced by her hostess to other well known Londoners - the Langtry's landlady was already complaining about the number of people coming to her house with invitation. One of the later invitations was from a friend of the Prince of Wales. He invited both the Prince and the Langtrys to one of his dinner parties. That meeting between Bertie - as the Prince was known to friends - and Lillie eventually led to her becoming his mistress for several years and to his continuing friendship right up to his death in 1910.

Meeting with Bertie, being presented to his mother, Queen Victoria, were obviously high points in Lillie's life but, unfortunately, there were low moments too. Edward Langtry's once handsome income from his Irish estates gradually diminished, so a cut back on their expenses was vital. Edward himself was also fast becoming a reclusive alcoholic, no longer wishing to share in Lillie's delight in London society.

Then, once Lillie's affair with Bertie was over, she met another Royal Prince - a distant cousin of Bertie's - Prince Louis of Battenburg. By him she had an illegitimate daughter who, much later gave Lillie a grand daughter - the television personality Mary Malcolm. But, by the time of Mary's birth in 1918 , Lillie had divorced Edward in 1887 and he had died a penniless alcoholic two years later. In 1899, for the second time, and again in St. Saviour's Church, Lillie married. Her second husband was Hugo de Bathe the eldest son of Sir Henry de Bathe.

They were, however, an ill matched couple and Hugo, on Lillie's recovery, spent most of his time apart from his wife in Nice.

Lillie, though, should not go down in history merely as one of the Royal mistresses, nor simply as the wife of two unsuccessful husbands. When she herself was down on her luck, when bailiffs invaded the little Norfolk Street house, and Mr Langtry frequently found it convenient to go fishing, 'leaving me to deal with the unwelcome intruders as best I could,' she depended entirely on her own efforts to improve her lot.

First of all, to earn an income, Lillie decided to take to the stage. After a shaky start, she eventually became a member of the famous Bancroft theatrical company, playing at the Haymarket in London in such parts as Shakespeare's Rosalind and his Cleopatra. Later she toured her own company, both America and South Africa. In fact, she became known as one of the hardest working actresses on the stage at that time.

Another of her ventures was to have stables in Newmarket. Here she bred race horses and raced there under the name of 'Mr Jersey.' She had her largest win ever - £120,000 - with her famous horse Merman who won the Cesarewitch in 1892. No wonder La Layette's portrayal of Lillie was captured by the sketch seven years later as: 'The goddess of Goodwood, Mrs Jersey.'

By 1900 Lillie was back in Jersey. She came to open St Helier's new Opera House, taking the female lead in 'The Degenerates', as well as delighting her fellow Islanders by speaking in Jersey Norman-French at the end of the play. Another six years and she had turned her back on the theatre proper and tried her hand at vaudeville in New York. But she still had time to become the first woman to break the bank of Monte Carlo!

What next? Lillie thought she would try writing a novel. The punning title she gave to the twenty-eight amusing chapters she wrote was 'All at Sea.' It brought her good reviews as being 'witty' and 'clever', plus £1,200 in royalties. Then, during The Great War, not only did she donate her own salary and any profits from staging 'Mrs. Thompson' at Drury Lane Theatre to the Red Cross, but she also gave benefit performances to the troops on both sides of the Atlantic.

On her retirement from both acting and as a race-horse owner, Lillie went to live in Monaco. There, in 1929, at the age of seventy-five, she died. Lillie was buried, as she wished, in St Saviour's churchyard, in the same grave as her parents and two of her brothers. Her white marble bust can still be seen there, looking towards the rectory, now known as 'La Belle Maison,' where she had lived such a full Jersey life with her six brothers.

SYBIL HATHAWAY - THE DAME OF SARK

Nearly 300 years after Helier de Carteret had Queen Elizabeth I's letters patent, allowing him to colonise Sark, the Collings family had the opportunity to buy the fiefdom of Sark. In 1927, the great grand-daughter of the first Dame of Sark in the Collings family herself became the Island's Dame and moved into the 17th century family house known as 'La Seigneurie.' With pride Sybil called herself 'a true Serquais' and promised to do all she could for the good and prosperity of her island. And that, during her forty-six years as Dame of Sark, is exactly what Sybil most certainly did.

As a child Sybil found Sark a wonderfully challenging place in which to grow up. Encouraged by her father, she loved swimming and climbing up cliffs, she knew how to use a gun to keep down the Island's rabbits; and she much enjoyed pitting her wits against the most obstinate of the donkeys she used to ride. So, just as growing up in Jersey had helped Lillie Langtry to become self reliant, growing up in Sark gave Sybil both the toughness and self-reliance she would later need.

Sybil's first major obstacle in life was her father's intense dislike of Dudley Beaumont, the man who wanted to marry her. He was so angry that he threw her out of 'La Seigneurie' in her nightdress. So, though she was only seventeen, the very next morning Sybil left Sark with Dudley. Once in London, they were married in St James' Church, Piccadilly. Eleven years later, however, they returned to Sark, when the family rift was healed and where they began to breed Guernsey cows.

Dudley served in the Great War in both France and Africa but, sadly, he died in the influenza epidemic of 1918. This tragic loss left Sybil with six children to bring up but with absolutely no help towards her expenses being offered by either Dudley's father or her own. So, in order to support herself and her children, she immediately began to look for work. She found it with the British Army of Occupation in Germany, at the Y.M.C.A. in Cologne. It was while working here that Sybil learned German, an accomplishment which was to stand her in such good stead during the Second World War.

In 1927 Sybil's father, the irascible William Collings, Sark's Seigneur, died. So, Sybil came back to her island and, in a special meeting of the Chief Pleas, took her place as the Dame of Sark. Once installed in La Seigneurie, Sybil found the family home, from which she had been banished twenty-six years earlier, in a terrible state of disrepair and in great need of modernisation. The house did not even have running water or a bathroom. With her customary energy, Sybil at once set about selling some of the family owned property in Guernsey and used the proceeds to make La Seigneurie more habitable and comfortable.

Though also trying to make amends for her father's neglect of Sark and fulfiling her duties as Dame - such as collecting her tithes, being patron of the Island's one living, plus being the sole keeper of pigeons and bitch dogs in Sark - Sybil still found time to fall in love. She accepted the proposal of marriage from a newcomer to Sark, Major Douglas James. To her astonishment the Vicar of Sark adamantly refused to marry the pair. He had recognised the so-called 'Major' as the man whose wedding he had taken seven years before in Singapore. Not only did Sybil's fiancé then hurriedly leave Sark, but he took with him the money given him by Sybil to pay bills for the family's property repairs. Back in the U.K., James was summoned to appear in court, charged with several cases of fraud and was sentenced to three years in prison.

There was, however, a happier outcome to the chance meeting of Sybil with the American born Robert Hathaway. This was in London when, after two years of setting both La Seigneurie and Sark to rights, Sybil was about to start on a well deserved holiday in America. Once she had returned from her American trip, she and Robert were married at St Marylebone's church in London.

On the couple's return to Sark, Robert took the title of Seigneur and shared the responsibility of looking after the interests of the Serquais with Sybil. She, in her turn, took advantage of her husband's American connections by going to the U.S. and giving Sark's attraction as a holiday destination greater publicity through her lecture tours.

Sybil's finest hour as Sark's Dame in her fellow Islanders eyes came when England declared war on Germany in 1939 and, after the fall of Dunkirk in 1940, offered all Channel Islanders the chance to evacuate the Islands, ships being provided for passage to the U.K. Sybil declared emphatically that she would be staying in Sark and called on all born Serquaise to follow her example. So she and her fellow Islanders were still there when on 28th June, 1940, several Sark fishing boats were fired on by German planes as they flew back to base after dropping bombs on both Jersey and Guernsey.

Four days later, after both Bailiwicks had surrendered to the Germans and the German occupation of the Islands had began, on 2nd July, a party of high-ranking German Officers landed in Sark. They were received at La Seigneurie by both Sybil and her husband. Immediately, recognising how well bred these German officers were, Sybil played up to their aristocratic notions and let drop in the conversation that her 'name and status' were included in the prestigious 'Almanach de Gotha.' So, throughout the nearly five years of German Occupation, whenever there was a problem in Sark that involved the enemy, rather than dealing with lower-ranking Germans, she always approached one of their aristocrats. She got on particularly well, to the benefit of all her fellow Islanders, with Baron von Aufsess and Prince Oettingen, though quite ready to tell them - in German - what their forces could and could not do in Sark.

So, who was it, in the desperate winter of 1944, when all food supplies from France had been cut off by the Normandy landings, who organised the Serquaise raid of a German grain stock? None other than the Dame of Sark herself. She also had had the foresight to hoard a secret cache of potatoes, which saved many a Sark family from starvation. Again, what happened after the liberation of the Channel Islands when British troops could not be spared to stay in Sark? Sark's Dame took immediate command of the Island's German garrison. Not only did she organise them in their general cleaning up of the Island, but she also instructed them to dispose of all the land mines they had planted against a British invasion.

After the Island's Liberation, Sybil had the honour of welcoming two Royal parties to Sark. In 1949 she and her husband welcomed Princess Elizabeth and the Duke of Edinburgh, who had come to open the new La Maseline harbour. Eight years later, Sark had an even greater honour, when the Royal couple returned after Elizabeth's accession as Queen. This made their second visit the first time in its whole history that a reigning monarch had set foot in Sark. A Ceremony of Homage, marking this unique occasion, took place during a special meeting of the Chief Pleas. After these two Royal visits, the Dame of Sark was first awarded the O.B.E and then, in 1965, a Dame Commander of the Order of the British Empire - or, as Sybil herself put it, the Queen made her a 'Double Dame.'

Yet, four years after this great honour, Sybil told Chief Pleas that she intended surrendering her Royal Charter - dating back to Helier de Carteret - to the Crown and giving Sark to Guernsey to govern. Why? This threat of 'abdication' came about because Sybil was disheartened by both the lax way Sark was being administered and the undisciplined behaviour of her fellow Islanders. She realised that their flouting of licensing and traffic laws were spoiling the good order and tranquillity Sark's visitors and residents had always enjoyed. Her announcement 'made the Sark people sit up and look into their affairs.' A tightening up of the Islander's observance of Sark's laws was put into immediate effect. The result was both a quieter, hooligan-free island to attract peace-loving visitors and the restoration of Sark's Dame - she agreed not to abdicate.

Dame Sybil Hathaway and her husband Robert were able to celebrate their silver wedding before he died just five weeks later. Sybil herself, after nearly fifty years of governing and caring for Sark, died in July, 1974. Her great loss to the Island was sincerely mourned by all of Sark's inhabitants

JOHN ARLOTT

With a mile long breakwater for yachts to shelter behind and the first Channel Islands airport in 1935 to be built - complete in 1968 with its own air service - Alderney has long been a favourite destination for both U.K. and French visitors. But, like the other islands in the Guernsey Bailiwick, Alderney has also attracted outsiders to stay on as residents. They appreciate the Island as a tranquil place in which to live; they know they will have the opportunity to enjoy such relaxing pleasures as sailing the eight miles to France, fishing, playing golf, studying the history of its twelve fortresses, or bird-watching - there is a puffin colony of about twenty thousand on the islet of Burhou alone.

Among the people who have settled in Alderney in the twentieth century some had already made their reputation before they arrived. So there was the author of 'The Sword in the Stone,' T.H. White, living in Royal

Connaught Square from 1947 to 1964; Elizabeth Beresford of 'The Wombles' farce, who still lives there; and, of course, the famous voice of cricket himself, John Arlott, who spent his last years near Longis Bay.

Leslie Thomas John Arlott, the only child of a metal repairer, was born in Basingstoke, Hampshire, on the 25th of February, 1914. It was not long before one of the many interests in his life surfaced. At the age of six he started to collect things. And what started this collecting habit? A free booklet given away with his favourite 'Rover' comic. And, to begin with, the craze also included collecting - in a tin box kept specially for the purpose - the bits of tickets punched by bus conductors. Perfect home made 'confetti.'

A more expected interest, plus talent, showed itself when we won a scholarship to the local grammar school, Queen Mary. Here he played opening bat not just for his house's cricket team, but also for the school's. It was here, too, that he was able to further his avid interest in reading, though, to John's disappointment, his English master was rather scathing about John's ambition to write poetry.

On leaving Queen Mary's School, John's first job, at the age of fifteen, was as an office boy in Hampshire Council's Planning Department - for £1 a week. But, after a few months, John happened to see an advert asking for a diet clerk to work at Park Prewett mental hospital for £2 a week. John applied for the job and, from 1930 to 1934, was responsible every morning for ordering the correct amount of food needed by the patients and staff for that day.

John's next job move, in 1934, was to enroll as a constable in Southampton's Police Force. He had noted, naturally, that it had a strong cricket team! He finally left the Southampton force in 1945, having had the privilege not only of being opening bat for them when off duty, but also, in 1938, of being picked as 12th man for one day for Hampshire's team. It was the peak of his cricketing career!

During those eleven years as a policeman, several other important events happened, including a lead into the career for which John Arlott is still best remembered. First of all, in 1940, he married Dawn Rees, a nurse at the Royal South Hampshire Hospital and they eventually moved, with their two sons, Jim and Tim, to Highgate in North London. From there, still wanting to further his schoolboy's ambition to write poetry, he sent a letter to the then almost unknown poet, John Betjeman. He simply asked whether Betjeman would be willing to collaborate with him on a book of topographical poetry.

The poet, however, was already committed to bringing out an anthology of his own, but nevertheless wrote back to John with words of encouragement. Then, in 1943, the long hoped for event happened; the topographical anthology, now called 'Land Marks,' selected by George Hamilton and John Arlott, was actually published and it included John's own poem 'Cricket at Worcester 1938'. Another ambition had been realised.

Next came John Betjeman's unexpected role in John's life. The poet happened to mention to a B.B.C. talks producer that he had recently been contacted by a policeman with a penchant for poetry. Geoffrey Grigson, the producer then wrote to John, asking whether he would give a radio talk about being a poetry loving policeman. Grigson's reaction after that broadcast? 'This man is a natural broadcaster and should be encouraged.'

It was with Grigson's own encouragement that John wrote his first script, 'The Hampshire Giants.' It was all about the 18th century village cricket club that between 1772 and 1796 defeated the English XI no fewer than 37 times. Not only did this talk captivate John's listeners, but, in 1945, it was published in full in 'The Listener' magazine.

So a poet's chance remark to the right person at the right time led to John Arlott becoming the B.B.C's best known (so easily recognisable by his distinctive Hampshire accent) and much loved cricket commentator.

His own excellent memory, keen observation, good humour, knowledge of cricket, plus a gift for using the English language with precision and panache, which were all so evident as he broadcast, earned him several awards. In 1970 there was his O.B.E.: in 1979 and 1980 he was voted Journalist of the Year and, in 1980 too, the Sports Presenter of the Year.

How did a cricket enthusiast also become a wine buff? In Sicily he absent-mindedly poured himself a glass of wine from a jug of what he thought was water sitting on the table. John drank his glass full, liked it and never after that drank a drop of beer or whisky again. Later, as seemed inevitable, he became a Fleet Street wine columnist.

John had always told the family that he would retire when he was sixty five. By the time he actually reached that age he had already, after seventeen years of marriage, divorced Dawn; had the tragedy of the deaths of first his eldest son and then his second wife, Valerie, to bear.

All he wanted now was to escape from England with his third wife, Pat, whom he had met at Lord's when she was working there as a secretary. Alderney had always been a favourite holiday destination for the whole family since his first visit there in 1951. It was no surprise, therefore, that while he, Pat, Tim and his third son, Robert, were staying in the Georgian Hotel in February 1980, that they all decided that Alderney would be the best place for John to retire to.

Once John had signed the contract for the 'The Vines,' he immediately thought of himself as a 'naturalised Aurignians' and soon found three excellent friends to keep him in good spirits now that he - a workaholic - had retired from all the work that had once meant so much to him. There was Yorkshireman, Geoff Rennard, the Polish André d'Aquinio, working in Alderney on his pottery statues of famous cricketers; and farmer Tim Morgan who enjoyed fishing and flying planes.

John himself continued to enjoy good wine and conversation and, in 1984, was only too happy to be a member of the 'Any Questions?' team when it came to Alderney. His scathing remarks about trade unionists in the 1980's, such as: 'The modern educational system scoops up all those with good brains and takes them away and it leaves those who can't pass their 'O' levels to be trades union leaders. If your intellect is thus limited and you have a chip on your shoulder you're not an ideal leader of working people!' showed that he still kept his finger on the pulse of U.K. politics and retained his way with words.

Another highlight of his time in Alderney was when the Guardian asked John to pick - and give reasons for his choice - his Desert Island Cricket team. In his team John had Jack Hobbs and Ted Dexter from England; Vivian Richards and Learie Constantine from the West Indies; and Keith Miller from Australia, as just five members of his fabulous XI.

He chose too, of course, the exciting new player, Ian Botham, who later on, when he flew to Alderney to visit John, decided he too would like to live there.

Other delights for John in Alderney itself were to be driven to the 'First and Last' restaurant in Braye Bay and eat oysters to the accompaniment of a bottle of Chablis. Another feature in the Island's favour, which John took advantage of was its proximity to Cherbourg. From there his friend Geoff Rennard once drove John down to Saint Emilion, where he was to receive a local award for his recognition of the qualities of St Emilion's wines.

There was, though, a downside to John's last years in Alderney. In 1985 his local doctor diagnosed bowel cancer and suggested that he go to the mainland for treatment. He was operated on at the Radcliffe Hospital in Oxford. To his family's surprise, however, he recovered so well, that the next day, with his well-known mischievous grin, he asked his wife and two sons, 'Have you got that Gravadlax and Chablis I asked for?'

A year later, though, came the next blow - he had a stroke. By now his ill health, and especially his chronic bronchitis, so limited his movements that his main exercise was to cross the road from the Vines and walk to where he could look across the sea, just as he said, to take 'a look at France to make sure it's still there!' He therefore relied on one of his two sons to drive him round the Island every afternoon.

It happened to be his third son, Robert's turn, when a nasty incident happened. Robert had just parked the car in the lay-by at Clonque Bay when three youths in a car drew up next to them. While one of the youths began cleaning his nails with a pointed knife, all of them started to make faces and jeer at John. Robert shouted at them to go away and then started to drive his father back to The Vines. When they were nearly there, the youths' car appeared from the opposite direction, turned round and began to chase the Arlott's car. Robert stopped and got out of the car, but two of the youths jumped up at him, punching him and cutting his face with a studded belt one of them had wrapped round his fist.

Thankfully, at that point, some golfers saw what was happening and stopped the whole frightening episode. Unfortunately, John was interviewed on Channel Television that night to find out from him exactly what had happened. Viewers were shocked to see how old and confused he seemed and the whole event was publicised further by the national press the next day.

A fall down his cellar steps in January 1990 was John's next misfortune and so serious was his condition that he had to be flown over to Southampton General Hospital. When he had recovered sufficiently, he returned to Alderney but, sadly, all he was able to do was sit in his wheelchair, looking as depressed as he so obviously felt.

It was in December 1991 that at last came John's release from his physical and mental pain. Only the evening before John had put one hand into each of his son's hands and said to them, 'I love you.'

His family, with John's last wishes in mind, set about arranging both the details of his memorial service in Hampshire and the funeral itself in Alderney. On John's headstone in St Anne's churchyard they decided to have inscribed in his memory the last two lines of John's poem in praise of the poetry written by the parson - poet, Andrew Young.

John's own validation of his long life of so many different achievements was: 'So clear you see these timeless things that, like a bird, the vision sings.'

The familiar image of Jim Bergerac, otherwise known as John Nettles

Chapter Four

The More Recent Famous

Go anywhere in the world and say 'Bergerac' and someone will nod and say: 'the Jersey detective.' But John Nettles who was granted qualifications to live in the Island, only actually did so for a short time.

JOHN NETTLES

John was raised in Cornwall and went to a local grammar school. He then went on to Southampton University to study History and Philosophy. He began his acting career in repertory and has spent most of his time 'treading the boards' all over England and Scotland. He toured the USA in 'The Hollow Crown' in 1981. John has been everyone from Abanazar in Aladdin to Julius Caesar in Antony and Cleopatra. He was also Robin Hood in a radio production.

On television John Nettles has performed in 'The Liver Birds,' 'The Merchant of Venice,' 'Family at War' and of course 'Bergerac,' which has been televised world-wide, and many would say that he put Jersey on the map. He has also worked extensively with the Royal Shakespeare Company.

An accomplished actor in every sense of the word, John has been in more productions than you could ever shake a truncheon at, the latest being

'Midsomer Murders' in which again he plays a cunning detective Chief Inspector, Tom Barnaby.

John has also written a few books: two of them about Jersey.

 He now lives near Eversham with his wife Cindy and his two dogs. He still makes the odd flying visit to Jersey to visit his daughter, Emma.

ALAN WHICKER

Broadcaster Alan Whicker, was best known for his 'Whicker's World' television series but, over the years, he has been involved in a large number of productions world-wide. He has travelled many thousands of miles and interviewed hundreds of people in the making of his unique style of Whicker 'doco.'

Born in 1925, Alan served as a Captain with the 8th Army during World War II. It is possible that during that time he learned his trade as a programme maker as he was involved in producing and directing several army films. After the war he worked as a foreign correspondent, and was war correspondent with the American 5th army in Korea.

He began his career in broadcasting with the BBC in 1957 and was a founder member of Yorkshire Television in 1968. Alan has been involved in the making of over a hundred documentaries and received eight prestigious awards for his broadcasting skills. In 1996 he did a series for BBC radio.

It is very convenient that listed amongst the things he likes to do are meeting people and photography. Alan, who now lives in Jersey, is also a writer with seven books to his credit. He enjoys reading, though, as he says, a lot of his reading involves airline timetables.

BRIAN WALDEN

Winning the 'Television Times Favourite TV Current Affairs Personality 1990' and 'ITV Personality of the Year 1991' must rank Brian Walden amongst the nation's most popular political presenters. Most who watched 'The Walden Interview' would no doubt agree.

Brian Walden was born in July, 1932. Both his parents had been married before so Brian had three elder step brothers. His education began at West Bromwich Grammar School before winning a scholarship to Queen's College Oxford. In 1957 he was elected President of the Oxford Union which stood him in very good stead for the future. He became in turn, a university lecturer, Labour MP for Birmingham All Saints for ten years from 1964 and Birmingham Ladywood for three years. He was also on the board of Central Television.

As a columnist, he wrote for the London Evening Standard, the Thomson Newspapers and The Sunday Times. Brian Walden's TV debut with London Weekend Television in 1986, heralded a string of successes including Shell International Award 1982, The Aims of Industry Special Free Enterprise Awards in 1990 and the BAFTA Richard Dimbleby award. His book: 'The Walden Interviews' was published in 1991.

One of his favourite pastimes is to play a hard fought game of chess whilst relaxing in his home in St Peter Port, Guernsey.

JACK HIGGINS

If you like to read an exciting, plausible, well researched tale, pick up any of the thirty to forty best sellers by Jack Higgins, or Harry Patterson or Henry Patterson or James Graham or Martin Fallon or even Hugh Marlow, odds are you won't put it down till the last gripping paragraph. Jack Higgins - whose real name is Harry Patterson - was born in Newcastle on July the 27th, 1929 but lived in Belfast until the age of eleven where his mother was from. He then moved to Leeds.

Educated at Poundhay School, Leeds, Beckets Park Teachers School and the London School of Economics. Jack (or Harry) had a very varied working life. From NCO in the Royal Horse Guards (serving on the East German border during the cold war) to clerk to a circus tent hand - then on to school master, lecturer and tutor, after taking degrees in sociology and social psychology.

He has been a full time author since around 1960 and has had many best selling and successful novels. Many of his books have been turned into films including 'The Violent Enemy,' which was banned for political reasons by the foreign office, 'The Wrath of God,' 'A Prayer for the Dying,' starring Bob Hoskins and Mickey Rourke, and 'Thunder Point', and of course 'The Eagle Has Landed.' Some of his books have been filmed for television, such as 'Night of the Fox,' 'Eye of the Storm' and 'On Dangerous Ground.' Others are still in production. His novels have sold over 250 million copies world-wide and have been translated into fifty-five different languages earning him an estimated £20 million.

He has lived and written in Jersey for over twenty five years and enjoys playing tennis and old movies. He is patron of the Jersey Film Society. Jack is twice married and has a son and three daughters.

TERENCE ALEXANDER

Devotees of the Bergerac television series will always remember Terence Alexander's excellent portrayal of Charlie Hungerford, Sergeant Bergerac's rather dodgy father-in-law who was also 'something' in local government - sort of a rich man's Arthur Daley. He was a familiar figure around Jersey for a number of years.

Though Terence never actually had formal dramatic training, his appearance on stage, television, in film and on radio, span nearly sixty years. He started out as assistant stage manager with 'The White Rose Players' in Harrogate in December 1939. Part of the job was to play any roles that hadn't been filled. Amongst the cast at that time were Dulcie Grey, Trevor Howard and Philip King.

Terence went on to do repertory in Sheffield and Leeds, then in January 1942, started in John Gielgud's Macbeth. However, as with so many people, Hitler and his war made a mess of his plans - his country needed him more than the stage did.

Drafted in to the Army, Terence served in the ranks before being sent to Sandhurst for officer training. After getting his commission he served with the 27th Lancers. In 1945, while in Italy, his career was nearly ended by the departing enemy.

1947, and with wounds healed, Terence Alexander is once again treading the boards in repertory up and down the country.

Television came next with live programmes from Alexander Palace (no relation). That was in 1951. From then on he made hundreds of TV appearances including the Forsythe Saga. His film career led him to make some sixty films, his favourite being 'The League of Gentlemen.' Terence starred in the several West End plays, and that well-known voice has also been heard in many a radio production.

OLIVER REED

If a man's early occupations include being a cab driver, a night club bouncer, a boxer and serving with the RAMC, what else is left but a brilliant career as a film actor!

Oliver Reed was born in Wimbledon in 1938 and educated at Ewell Castle. His film debut came in 1960 when he played Mick in 'The Angry Silence.' Reed has appeared in more than fifty films including, 'Oliver' where he played the evil Bill Sykes. The totally different character he portrayed in 'Women in Love' showed his versatility, though he did seem to get cast in the brooding, dangerous mold - well, I suppose you wouldn't have really gone out of your way to kick sand in his face!

Amongst his other achievements, Oliver Reed wrote an autobiography: 'Reed All About Me.' The book 'The Films of Oliver Reed,' written in 1975 by Susan d'Arcy is a must for fans.

Oliver Reed died on May the 2, 1999 in Malta during the filming of 'Gladiator,' in which he turned in a powerful final performance.

GILBERT O'SULLIVAN

Raymond Edward O'Sullivan was born in Eire in 1946 but went to school in Swindon. He began composing songs whilst at art college in the swinging sixties. As he became known in the music world he took the stage - or bandstand name - of Gilbert O'Sullivan. This was of course a little confusing for the more traditional Gilbert and Sullivan devotees.

He composed and performed dozens of numbers including three number ones in the hit parade, including 'Nothing Rhymes' and 'Clair.'

Gilbert also cut eight albums and received eight awards including 'Best Song of the Year,' 'Best Songwriter of the Year' and in 1973, the 'Million Performance Award' for 'Alone Again, Naturally.' He has lived in Jersey for several years. Hopefully not alone.

ROBERT FARNON

Robert Farnon who now lives in Guernsey, wrote his first serious piece of music at the age of twelve. Born in 1917, he was brought up in Toronto, Canada, with three brothers and two sisters. It was at the Broadus Farmer School of Music that he learned to play trumpet. Robert Farnon's first symphony was performed in 1941.

During his musical career he arranged and conducted for Vera Lynn, Bing Crosby, Tony Bennet and many more. It was André Previn who described him as 'the greatest arranger in the world.' Robert composed hundreds of pieces of light music in his time, plus the background music for many film epics and television productions. He received five awards and commendations and it was said that his skill and enthusiasm when handling an orchestra were 'a delight to hear and behold.'

An indication of his musical skill - and the fact that he may have been ambidextrous - can be found in the story of how, in his early days as a trumpet player with Percy Faith, he would play his trumpet with his left hand whilst holding a pencil in the right, then every time he had a few bars 'rest' he would be busy writing arrangements!

GERALD DURRELL
Gerald Durrell loved animals, all animals, big, small, four legs, two legs or none at all. He loved them - even spindly insects or eight legged beasties. After leaving India where he was born in 1925, he was educated on the continent by private tutors. This education was to influence his life more than most, as the emphasis was on natural history.

He became a student keeper at Whipsnade Zoo in 1945. When he was twenty-one, he inherited £3000. This enabled him to realise an ambition. Leading and financing his own expedition, Gerald Durrell took off for little known corners of the world to collect zoological specimens. Many of his finds were gratefully received by zoological gardens in America and Europe. He was also able to contribute twenty-two new species to the London Zoological Society.

In 1959 he created a zoological park in Jersey. Then, in 1963, he founded the Jersey Wildlife Preservation Trust of which he was honorary director. The trust, which took over from the zoo park, is mainly concerned with the captive breeding of endangered species and conservation.

In 1973, Gerald Durrell established Wild Life Preservation International in the USA and, twelve years later, he did the same in Canada. Both these organisations are mainly concerned with raising funds to help cover the very high running costs of the Jersey preservation trust. More than twenty five thousand members receive a regular newsletter. There are facilities for research and training at the zoo.

The several hundred overseas students who have received training here will have gained much knowledge of mammal, bird and reptile. During their stay they will also have gained knowledge of the shovel and the bucket.

Gerald Durrell wrote over thirty books which were translated into twenty-six different languages. He received the OBE in 1983. The name of the trust has now been changed to The Durrell Wildlife Preservation Trust in memory of that very special man. His widow, Lee Durrell, is carrying on the great work.

IAN BOTHAM

Ian Botham could almost be called Mister Cricket - and he has an OBE to prove it! Born on November the 24th, 1955, in Cheshire, he was educated, and no doubt introduced to his first innings - at Milford School Cheshire.

As right handed batsman and a medium fast bowler, Ian had his debut with Somerset in 1974, and in 1976 he gained his county cap. He has 'played the game' and 'kept a straight bat' all over the world, including New Zealand, India, Pakistan and Australia, and was England Captain 1980/81.

In the course of his career Ian Botham has ruffled a few feathers but he has also attained some very impressive records. He was first to score a century and to take eight wickets in the same innings. He played in over one hundred test matches, scored more than five thousand runs and assisted the return to the pavilion of nearly six hundred dispirited batsmen.

Between innings Ian has written three books, including an autobiography. He is fond of shooting, golf, flying and fishing. He also gave a very professional performance in a TV commercial promoting Alderney where he lives and more recently Shredded wheat.

GRAEME LE SAUX

Graeme Le Saux, Jersey's own bit of football pride, was born on October 17th, 1968. He was educated at Hautlieu and d'Hautrée. He lived for football and kept fit by running and cycling.

Graeme played for St Paul's FC. Later followed in his father's footsteps as a Muratti player. He was selected to join the England 'B' under 21s. In his early twenties he joined Chelsea Football Club as an apprentice; it was not the happiest of times for Graeme. Later he joined Blackburn Rovers where he found a much friendlier atmosphere. More recently he rejoined Chelsea which he was delighted to find had altered considerably.

His skill during his many league appearances led to him being selected to play in the England team on twenty three occasions. During the 1998 World Cup Graeme played an excellent game, as did his team mates, despite being reduced to ten men.

Back at his best during the 2001/2 season, Graeme turned in a fine performance for Chelsea. By the start of the 2002/3 season he had played a total of 278 games, scoring fourteen goals along the way. In 2002 he also received an FA Cup runners up medal.

MATT LE TISSIER

Matt Le Tissier was born in Guernsey just three days before Jersey's Graeme Le Saux and is considered by many to be one of the best English football players today but he does seem to be plagued by ill chance.

Matt's genius was discovered while he was playing for Guernsey club, Vale Recreation. Three days after his eighteenth birthday, he was signed up for England 'B.' In his first season with Southampton he scored six goals in twenty four appearances and in the 1989-90 and 1990-91 seasons he put in an amazing thirty-nine goals!

He seemed to slow down a bit during the following two years but 1993 saw a return to even greater heights with forty-four goals in two seasons. Matt has been 'Player of the Year' at Southampton three times – and that is an official record. In three hundred games he scored an average of one goal every two games.

The trouble is that occasionally his batteries just seemed to run down, sometimes during a crucial game. Luck is not always with him either, like getting picked for England just as he receives an injury. For these reasons, despite all he has achieved, he only (only?) won eight England caps and was not been picked for the England squad – there are many people who are certain that he should have been included. Presumably, Manchester United and Chelsea who have made bids for him, and Southampton who refused to 'sell' him for £10m would agree.

During the 2001/2 season, he was plagued by injuries and at the end of the season, he decided to hang up his boots and enjoy a well earned retirement.

DEREK WARWICK

Derek Warwick enjoys being at home in Jersey with his wife Rhonda and their daughters, Marie and Kerry. If he is not at home, you may find him on the golf course doing battle with his handicap. Of course, he does have to look after the day job as well. Derek is co-owner of a car dealership and an investment vehicle management company - Derek Warwick International. So what else would this home loving, forty four-year-old do with his time?

Well, in 1990 he became number one driver for Lotus, and was one of the most respected Formula One drivers driving with Toleman in 1981. Later he was with Renault and then Brabham. 1987 was the start of three years with Arrows. He finished the season as highest ranked British driver - then he joined Lotus. 1998 saw him burning rubber in the British Touring Car Championship.

During a highly successful career in the hot seat Derek was also involved in stock car racing. He took the English, British and World championships.

His racing days began on Karts when he was twelve. By coincidence, Formula One team boss Eddie Jordon also started out with Kart racing, but this was thirty years ago at Jersey's Belle Vue when he spent a couple of seasons working in local bars.

NIGEL MANSELL

Nigel Mansell who has a home in Jersey, began his racing career on Karts in 1969. Between then and 1976 he won eleven regional championships, thus setting the seal on his future.

Born on August 8th, 1953, Nigel was educated at Wellsbourne and Hall Green Bilateral Schools, plus Polytechnics in Solihull, Bolton and Birmingham. He became an apprentice engineer with Lucas and later, a lab technician. When he was promoted to product manager, it is interesting to note that this champion world class racing driver of the future was senior sales engineer of the tractor division! In 1976 he left the tractors far behind and began driving Formula Ford and Formula Three. Three years race by and he goes from Formula Two to Formula One in 1980.

Nigel was with Lotus for a year before joining the Williams and later the Ferrari teams. From 1980 to 1994 he won a record thirty Grands Prix, earning him nearly £8m. In 1991 he slowed down just long enough for the Queen to present him with an OBE. – but Her Majesty did have to move quite smartly!

In 1992 Nigel Mansell OBE was Formula One World Drivers Champion, and American IndyCar Champion the following year.

He has written (with Derek Allsop): 'Driven To Win' in 1988 and 'Mansell & Williams, The Challenge for the Championship' in 1992. He also wrote (with Jeremy Shaw) 'Nigel Mansell's IndyCar Racing.' And 'Nigel Mansell, My Autobiography' (with James Allen).

To relax, he likes nothing better than driving – a ball around the golf course. Nigel Mansell OBE has a financial interest in the Woodbury Park Golf and Country Club. He is married with two children and has £35m stowed in the back of the garage behind the oil drum of his Jersey residence.

NIGEL BENN

When Nigel Benn joined the British Army in 1980, little did he realise that this was the start of two careers. During his Army service - which lasted five years - he saw service in West Germany and Northern Ireland. At the same time he was encouraged to box, that was the beginning of his career as a Middleweight.

Nigel Benn was ABA National Champion in 1986 with forty eight wins in forty nine fights. In 1987 he turned professional and from then till

1996 he 'stung like a bee' in more than a dozen fights.

He earned several awards and accolades during this time, from 'Best Young Boxer' to fourth 'Most Destructive Puncher in the World.'

Nigel who lives in Jersey, is married to Sharon. They have two sons and a daughter. He likes to keep fit and he is also fond of music. In fact he cut a single disc, 'Stand up and Fight,' which was released in 1990. He recently re-appeared in the public eye when he appeared in the reality game show, 'I'm a Celebrity Get Me Out Of Here!'

IAN WOOSNAM MBE

Ian Woosnam was born in Oswestry, England, close to the Welsh border in March 1958. However, ignoring that bit of the geography books, he decided that he was a Welshman.

Ian became a professional golfer in 1976. It took time for him to be noticed but when in 1982 he finished eighth in the European order of merit, he was on his way. 1983 was also a good year for Ian as he married Glendryth Mervyn Pugh – they have three children.

In 1987 he helped the European Ryder Cup team to victory. He won the Hong Kong Open and then took five wins in Europe. Ian was now into serious prize money. He was also the first British player to win the World Match-play Title.

Although he is not a particularly big man, Ian is known as one of the longest hitters in the game. This together with his tenacity and determination to win ranks him as one of the world's top players.

Then came the U.S. Masters. It was a nail-biting finish, everything was hanging on the last stroke, a six foot putt. Not the easiest, but 'Woosie's' Welsh wizardry and English nerve were ready for the task.

He played, he sunk it, he won the 1991 U.S. Masters. A year later at the age of thirty-four, he was awarded the M.B.E.

He wrote 'Ian Woosnam's Masterpieces' in 1988 and 'Power Golf' in 1989 with a new edition two years later.

Living in Jersey, it is easy for Ian to indulge his favourite pastimes, snooker, water-skiing, shooting and of course golf – sometimes with fellow millionaire Stan Thomas.

Ian Woosnam MBE, has around £15m buried in a bunker.

ANTHONY JACKLIN CBE

Tony Jacklin began playing golf in 1953. By 1991 he had written three books on the subject. He has been awarded the CBE and the OBE and is widely acknowledged as one of Britain's finest post war golfers.

Happily married, he has a daughter and two sons. Sadly, his wife Vivian died in 1988. Later he married Astrid and gained another son plus a stepson and a stepdaughter.

As a professional golfer since 1962, Tony won twenty-four tournaments world-wide. He played in seven Ryder Cup matches and was Captain of the Ryder Cup team.

Living in Jersey, he often played on La Moye course with Tommy Horton. It was here that they both took a young local player under their wing. Thus Wayne Stephens became a world class professional golfer.

Tony lived in Jersey for about six years during the seventies but has since moved to America.

TOMMY HORTON MBE

In 1940 the forces of Nazi Germany were advancing rapidly across France. Mrs. Horton decided that Jersey might not be the safest place for her family. Thus it was that young Tommy was born in Lancashire a year later.

As soon as the war ended the family returned to the Island. Tom went to Grouville Central School and later to Hautlieu. At the age of ten he joined the Jersey Eastern Golf Club where his progress as a golfer soon became evident. At the tender age of sixteen, he climbed out of the bunker and joined the Royal Jersey as an Assistant Professional to C.T. Tudor. Two years later he swung the job of Head Assistant Professional to W.T.Twine at Ham Manor Golf Club in Sussex.

It is not always a pipe dream that one day one will be 'discovered.' Tommy Horton's dream came true in 1964 when a wealthy London business man helped him become one of the celebrated 'Butten Boys.' Now that he was out of the rough and able to play the professional golf circuit, there was no holding him back. He gained second position in the 1967 Order of Merit and he had a major success at the RTV International in 1968.

After more than a dozen international wins and a place in the Ryder Cup team of 1975, Tommy, his wife Helen and their two children came home to Jersey. He was on the fairway again with the Ryder Cup team of 1977 and captained the British P.G.A in 1978. Over his career, Tommy won an incredible 23 senior tour titles.

He founded the first Young Professionals School and, in 1985, became the chairman of the Professional Golfers Association European Tour Committee.

Tommy was awarded the MBE in 2000, and he remains a renowned coach, course designer and broadcaster.

RON HICKMAN

If you are a Do-It-Yourself fiend, it's pretty certain that you are the proud owner of a 'Workmate' portable bench. At the very least you will have heard of it. But do you know the story behind it? If you are leaning comfortably on your bench, I'll tell you about Ron Hickman.

Ron was born on October 21st, 1932 in Natal, South Africa. He studied music and worked for the Department of Justice. Next he is with the Ford Motor Co. in Dagenham, employed as a model maker and stylist. 1957 saw him with Lotus Cars Ltd. as a development engineer, rising to become Design Director. During his time with Lotus he was the principal designer of the Elan and Europa sports cars.

He retired in 1968 to become an inventor full time but, before that, as a consultant, he had designed the principal seating for two lounges on the QE2!

The odd thing is, Ron Hickman is self taught - he had no formal training in design or engineering whatsoever. He is that rare breed, a natural born designer and inventor. When he invented the Workmate, none of the tool manufacturers were interested. However Ron had great faith in his invention and he wasn't giving up - he began marketing it himself. After four difficult years, Black and Decker opened their eyes and their wallets and decided to take it up.

Over thirty million Workmates have been sold world-wide. Not bad for an invention thought to be a non-starter.

Ron has now given up on inventing things but the money he gained from his brain wave has enabled him to design and build his dream house. This amazing dwelling appeared on a Jersey postage stamp in 1987 and is packed full of gadgets and gismos which remotely control just about everything in the house - with the exception of his wife Helen!

ELIZABETH BERESFORD

Most people connect Elizabeth Beresford's name with those charming woolly creatures 'The Wombles.' Reputedly, they live in Womblegarten on Wimbledon Common where they are under the strict eye of Miss Adelaide and Great-Uncle Bulgaria.

Miss Beresford, who in fact is Mrs. Robertson – married to Max Robertson the BBC commentator - is a prolific writer and broadcaster. Her ninety books include historical romantic and gothic novels as well as tales enjoyed by children of all ages! Elizabeth's unstoppable quill has also produced musicals, two films and one hundred and sixty television programmes. She inherited her love of writing from her father, J. D. Beresford, the novelist.

Born in 1926, Elizabeth attended St Mary's Hall in Kemptown and the Brighton and Hove High School. She became a freelance journalist and around 1948 began to break into the book market. Some readers may recall the lyrics of the Beatles' number which referred to 'The Wombles of Wimbledon' – that's fame!

Elizabeth Beresford now lives in Alderney where she is co-founder, with Betty Cherrett, of the Alderney Youth Trust. A lot of time is spent travelling and talking to children but The Wombles are not forgotten.

The Womble family who were sometimes visited by distant cousins from America and of course by Highlander MacWomble, are making the acquaintance of yet another relative, one of the Alderney Wombles. Young Bungo Womble is quite excited about this – or he would be if he could stay awake long enough!

With so much to occupy her, Elizabeth still finds time to wander out with her camera, enjoy a swim or entertain her friends – she keeps the garden tidy as well!

Sir Jessie Boot founded the now ubiquitous Boots the Chemists. This is the Jersey Queen Street branch

SIR JESSIE BOOT (LORD TRENT)

Young Jessie Boot learned a lot from his mother about old country remedies and cure-alls made from herbs, leaves or boiled roots.

Inheriting a small back street shop in Nottingham gave him the opportunity to put his knowledge to good use. He used to crush and mix these potions and, when required, boil them on the hob in his mother's kitchen. These medications were then dispensed over the counter to grateful customers. This was the very first 'Boots The Chemist' – the first in an empire that would include around thirteen hundred shops and give employment to some seventy thousand people - and earn him a title.

Born in 1850, the son of a farm labourer, he had what it takes to succeed in business. Total dedication and the ability to spot a gap in the market and find a way of filling it – at a profit. Jessie was a man who made his own decisions and seldom accepted ideas that were not his own.

As the chain of chemist shops grew, so did the pressures. By the time he was thirty five, the strain had become too much and he was forced to take a break – he took his break in Jersey.

It was here that he met, fell in love with and married Florrie Rowe, the vivacious twenty three year old daughter of a book seller. Florrie was a determined young lady and proved an excellent business partner. She instigated the selling of stationery, books and artist's materials in his stores. She instituted the Boots Library - with red sticks on books in which the language or descriptions might prove to be too strong for the gentle reader! She also held the unofficial role of mediator between the staff and her husband who could at times be rather abrupt. The empire grew and in 1924, Mr. and Mrs. Boot moved to Jersey where they bought Villa Millbrook. They became Lord and Lady Trent in 1928.

When Jessie Boot died in 1931, Lady Florence had the old Chapel at Millbrook completely refurbished in his memory. With the help of Réné

Lalique of Paris, the unique 'Glass Church' was created and became one of the show pieces of the island. She also donated to the people a piece of land which runs down to Victoria Avenue from opposite Villa Milbrook. It was 'For the young to play and the old to rest' – it became Coronation Park. And in 1933, Florence Boot opened the thousandth Boots store.

Someone else who was grateful to Lady Trent was a lad called Billy Butters. Before the war he had a great ambition to become a vocalist for popular songs and dance band work – what was known in those days as a crooner. He had the voice but he desperately needed help to finance a bit of extra tuition before his break into Show-Biz. Lady Trent sponsored him. He became very well known and, in gratitude, he changed his name to Bruce Trent.

Chapter Five
Some of the Island's Multi-Millionaires

It has been said that in the Channel Islands there are on average four millionaires per square mile. To be classed a millionaire one must own assets to that amount whether it be in cash, land, property, shares, art treasures and so on. Many of those already mentioned in the famous section are multi-millionaires in their own right like Nigel Mansell, Jack Higgins, Ian Woosnam and Ron Hickman among others - and there are far too many rich in the Islands to mention them all.

Most of the people we are about to take a lighthearted brief look at were included in the 2003 rich lists of the *Sunday Times* and *Daily Mail*. They are at the top of the tree and our estimates are based on various sources including the *Jersey Evening Post* and those financial whiz kids at the *Financial Times*. They are estimates only based on the assets already mentioned and are a bench-mark because the fortunes in most cases will vary as some assets, bank deposits, etc. are not included or available for obvious reasons. Also the financial dealings of these entrepreneurs and business-minded elite mean their fortunes will change regularly, sometimes on a daily basis.

If you were given a million pounds tomorrow and put it in the bank you would earn approximately £8,000 per month in interest, so now your only worry would be how to turn it into a multi-million or what to

Eye catching supercars are common on Island roads. Models like this Ferrari are more likely to be paid for with cash than by hire purchase!

spend it on. Here is a summary of what the real millionaires have spent it on, and how they made it in the first place.

DAVID AND JONATHAN ROWLAND (660M)
(Finance)

The son of a scrap dealer, David Rowland scored his first million at the tender age of twenty-three by developing property. By the eighties, his worth had risen to £100m, with shrewd investments in oil, shipping and casinos.

David's son, Jonathan has followed in his father's footsteps. He sold his internet investment company, Jellyworks, for a breathtaking £65m when the dotcom phenomenon was booming. Based in Guernsey, David is bringing a small company called Resourceworks (which will invest in natural resources such as oil) to the stockmarket.

According to the Sunday Times 2003 Rich List, David and Jonathan Rowland are officially the richest residents in the Channel Islands.

SIR DAVID AND SIR FREDERICK BARCLAY   (650M)
(Property, media and hotels)

It is not often that a couple of lads start out as painters and decorators and are millionaires before they reach retirement age but that is the fantastic story of the Barclay twins, David and Frederick. From decorating they moved on to become estate agents and soon branched out into property development. It is this which so intrigues the media and makes their every move newsworthy.

However, the Barclay brothers prefer privacy and do not welcome publicity. Possibly for this reason they bought an island and furnished it as a £40m impregnable fortress. They wouldn't go so far as to pour boiling oil down from the battlements but nosy-parkers and 'rubber necks' are not welcome on the Channel Island of Brechou.

In 1991, in a sense, they joined the media with the purchase of The European newspaper. Later they became owners of The Scotsman and The Scotsman on Sunday. David and Frederick Barclay also own several prestigious hotels including the London Ritz. In 1994 they bought a motor retailer - The Automotive Financial Group - for £200m. Their purchase of the Littlewoods mail order company for £750m was a shrewd investment: financial experts say it could be worth a billion. They have also profited from forays into property development, hotels, car finance and shipping. In 1999, the twins made £200m by backing Philip Green's takeover of the Sears Group.

As with any business empire they have, at times, suffered losses running into millions of pounds (for example, the famous Ritz lost them £2.4m in 2001) but their huge assets and financial wizardry have helped to keep £650m stashed away in the castle dungeon.

The most important thing they own, as far as Channel Islanders are concerned, is the Barclay Brothers' helicopter, which they readily make available to assist at any emergency in the area. Thanks chaps.

JACK & FRED WALKER AND FAMILY(650M)
(Steel, aviation and property)

Jack Walker was born in Lancashire in 1931. On leaving school he entered his father's sheet metal company, C.Walker & Sons, with his elder brother, Fred. When their father died in 1951 the brothers inherited the family business. Together they developed their steel stock holding trade into a leading force. In 1989, the Walkers sold out to British Steel for a tidy £330m. Jack Walker had been living in Jersey as a tax exile since 1970. This decision was apparently made by tossing a coin - one of the many available!

He then invested £40m in Jersey European Airways, later to become British European Airways and then Flybe. It went from success to success and is now one of the largest independent airlines in Britain, although it has recently suffered a £10m loss as the result of the events of 9/11.

A dream came true for Jack when he was able to invest the sum of £100m in his beloved Blackburn Rovers Football Club. Whether they ever let him play is not revealed - but after all, it was his ball.

Sadly, Jack Walker passed away in August 2000 aged seventy-one. His brother Fred has now assumed the mantle of head of the family. The family property portfolio is worth an impressive £70m and includes The Walker Industrial Park in Blackburn, where Fred Walker now lives.

WILLIAM JOHNSON (495M)
(Inventions)
William Johnson utilises the Channel Islands as a base for dreaming up his incredibly profitable inventions. His latest brainwave is the 'C-Bag', which keeps holed vessels afloat, thus preventing damage to shipping containers and their contents.

Johnson's company, DTL, should receive royalties of up to £10m in 2003, and his 70% stake in the company is worth an extraordinary £495m.

THE CLARKE FAMILY   (400M)
(Property)
The late Fred Clarke was the chairman of C. Le Masurier & Co., and a well known figure in Jersey. He was at one time Constable of St Helier - head man of the Honorary Police in the Parish. The family firm own more than twenty pubs throughout the Island, a large cash and carry wines and spirits complex plus some very valuable land in the centre of

Executive jets are among the many privately owned aircraft on standby to transport rich residents to business meetings overseas

St Helier, as well as a string of retail outlets and hotels.
The Clarke family are now the largest private landowners in Jersey.

Since the death of head of the family, Fred Clarke, in 2001, the family has sold C Le Masurier, and financial experts expect their fortunes to soar even higher in the future as their assets are re-organised.

STEVE MORGAN   (312M)
(Construction and leisure)

Steve Morgan founded a small engineering firm, Redrow Construction in 1974 with £5,000 borrowed from his father, and later branched out into construction. The 1980s saw a boom in house building and Redrow expanded and developed till, in 1994, the company was floated, valued at £298m. A good time to sell, but retaining a 40% share holding. He also owns a £43m holding in the De Vere leisure group.

Steve is a keen Liverpool fan. In fact he is keen to the tune of a net £8m stake - that's keen.

Steve Morgan bought Trinity Manor in Jersey for £5.5m and held the ancient title of Seigneur of the Manor, where he lived his retirement in style. His recent divorce lost him a good few million, but he still has around £312m in his counting house.

DAVID MURRAY   (267M)
(Football, property and industry)

David Murray started his own business at the age of twenty-three. Just a year later he lost his legs in a car crash - but even that couldn't stop him. He is now fifty-one and Murray International Holdings, which trades in property, electrical retailing and steel stockholdings saw a £5m profit on £220m sales in the year to January 2002 and is expecting £7.5m profit on £245m sales in 2002-2003. Murray International Holdings is worth around £175m, of which Murray has a healthy 82% stake.

His stake in Rangers Football Club paid a handsom dividend. He was able to sell 25% of his share for £40m and still retains shares worth £37m, although he is no longer chairman. David lives in St. Brelade, Jersey and has £200m buried in the penalty area.

DAVID CROSSLAND (192m)
(Travel)

In 1963 an ex-Burnley Grammar School lad started work as coffee boy at a Travel Agents. They say that coffee keeps you awake and travel broadens the mind. Well, young David Crossland must have been very wide-awake indeed, and certainly had an eye on broader horizons. Less than twenty years later, with the backing of his brother-in-law, Thomas Trickett, he bought his first travel agency. He became the Chairman of Airtours, which he bought in 1982 and became the world's largest tour operators. David Crossland always took a great pleasure in getting holiday makers to more exotic places at less exotic prices! In its heyday, Airtours (now called 'MyTravel') took a million and a half people on holiday and was cited as pioneering mass market tourism. He resigned from MyTravel in February, 2003. David is a Jersey resident and has £192m neatly packed in his flight bag.

STANLEY & PETER THOMAS   (190M)
(Property and airports)

Working in a bakery is, no doubt, a good way of learning to make bread, Forty years on, Stanley and Peter Thomas have undoubtedly made a great deal of bread. Some £190m is hidden away in the oven and the dough is rising nicely.

The brothers started their working life in the family run bakery business in South Wales. When it was sold they stayed on with the new owners for a while before starting out on their own as 'Peter's Savoury Products.'

Leisure and sport are part of the daily routine of many residents

A large boat in a marina is one of the better examples of conspicuous consumerism.

These proved very savoury indeed and, after eighteen years, they sold out to Grand Met for £75m and entered the property market.

They became leading lights in TBI, a London based property group, and with the aid of expert managers, their assets rose from £40m to £435m in ten years. They also operate airports in London, Cardiff, Belfast, and Orlando. However, since the tragic events of 9/11, profits have fallen steeply in the airline industry. The brothers' stake in TBI has fallen to £55m, but their other wise investments and assets mean that their place in the Rich List is still assured.

Stanley is still chairman of TBI but lives in Jersey where he loves a game of golf, often with Ian Woosnam. Stanley Thomas is another open handed millionaire, the 'crumbs that fall from his table' are worth at least £200,000 per year to worthy causes.

ROGER NORMAN (150M)
(Shipping)

The Commodore Group, a Channel Island shipping business established in 1947, was majority owned by Guernsey based businessman Roger Norman and his family, until 2002, when it was sold for £180m Norman's fortune is now estimated at around £150m, making him a formidable new entry in the Sunday Times 'Rich List.'

BRIAN DE ZILLE AND FAMILY (135M)
(Knitwear and health clubs)

When Brian de Zille and his wife Vera sat and froze on a Jersey beach during a miserable May twenty years ago, they probably weren't thinking about buying hotels or having a luxury office in the middle of St Helier. Chances are, trying to keep warm was more on the agenda. Despite that slight blip in Jersey's usually impeccably behaved weather, they still loved the place. Now after living here for at least three years, they still do.

In 1973 Brian de Zille founded The Sweater Shop retail chain and in 1995 he sold his 80% stake for £120m. But not just like that - a reasonable amount of graft did go on during those intervening years! The de Zille family have wide interests in Europe, including property in Spain and, of course Jersey. Their interests include The Lobster Pot and Club Carrefour - so presumably they can get a quick snack wherever they are in the Island. Failing that, Brian's £6m jet can whisk them off to just about anywhere, and back, quite quickly. The 'and back' part is very important, as he loves to be able to get home if at all possible.

Home, to Brian, Vera, Graham and Alison is perhaps one of the most beautiful houses in Jersey, situated in St. Lawrence. It was once owned by author Jack Higgins, which occasionally causes confusion to tourists and amusement to the family.

Recently Brian gave a donation to the Opera House Appeal. The family, including son Graham and daughter in law Alison, are taking a great interest in Jersey heritage and are keen to be involved in Jersey life. The family are currently embarking on developing a chain of health clubs in the Island.

Brian is a very private person. He shuns publicity and just likes to be 'one of the crowd' - with the number of millionaires living in the Island, it could be said that he's got his wish!

PHYLLIS SOMERS (120M)
(Inheritance)

Some people can boast that they own a private aeroplane - but it is not many who can claim to have owned an airport. In May 1997 Nat Somers died at the age of eighty-eight. At the time of his death he and his wife Phyllis were worth £120m - but Nat was worth more than just money. He was an astute investor, a hard bargainer and a shrewd dealer.

Professional interior decorators have made their mark
transforming the homes of wealthy individuals in the Islands

He and his wife lived in Jersey and, in the five years up to 1992, they received dividends worth £68m but money isn't everything.

Nat Somers was passionate about anything to do with flying. He learned to fly in 1936. He owned Southampton airport until 1988, when he sold it for a cool £50m. In 1955 he designed his own plane and, in 1995 he bought a jet at a cost of £22m. He also made many shrewd and lucrative property investments in Jersey.

Nat's widow, Phyllis, now eighty-one, has recently donated a considerable amount towards the newly built Somers Cancer Research Centre at Southampton University.

TOM SCOTT AND FAMILY (120M)
(Crane hire, energy and car sales)
Timothy and Tom Scott founded the Scott-Greenham Heavy Lifting Contractors in Nottingham, which evolved from their father's motor firm. Obviously lots of heavy objects needed to be lifted as, in 1985, the business was floated. Two years later they sold out to BET for £75m and moved to Jersey with their 46% share: £34.5m. Tom only intended to stay in Jersey for six months but he has been there ever since.

Tom chairs the International Energy Group, parent company of Jersey Gas, is chairman of Jacksons Ltd., and in June 1998 was appointed chairman of Channel Television. He is one of the most prominent businessmen in the Islands, with interests in three major Jersey based businesses: CI Traders, International Energy and Comprop, worth around £50m in total

Secluded houses with extensive grounds are available for prices in excess of £1 million but only after a prospective buyer has been awarded the necessary 'qualifications'

JOE MOORE   (100M)
(Industry)

As one door opens, so does another. So found Joe Moore when he founded the WMS group which designs and distributes window and door hardware. In 1993 Joe saw his window of opportunity and sold out to Sheffield Insulations for £53m. He took his 60% share of £32m and brought it over to Jersey, where his mansion was recently put up for sale at for £10m. This cash, together with his investments in the Far East, mean that pundits reckon he has £100m tucked away under the doormat.

DAVID KIRCH   (100M)
(Property)

David Kirch's age and fortune had something in common on his sixtieth birthday. Sixty years and sixty million!

This tidy bundle was mainly acquired by astute developing and letting of properties in and around London. in the sixties. In 1988, tiring of city life, he sold his last properties in the UK and retired to peaceful Jersey.

David still keeps his hand in as owner of Channel Hotels and Properties. They in turn have a £2.5m stake in Queensborough Leisure. Overall, David Kirch has net assets of around £39m in British based firms, and £46m of assets in Jersey.

Kirch's fortune looks set to increase even further, as he recently took many assets of the hands of recently bankrupted billionaire, Kevin Leech, at knock down prices.

DAVID SEYMOUR AND FAMILY (80M)
(Hotels)

David Seymour's family started out running guesthouses in Jersey in 1919. Almost a century later and the family own four of Jersey's biggest hotels: the Merton, Pomme d'Or, De La Plage and Portelet, at a total worth of around £40m. Their travel firm and other investments push their total fortune up to £80m.

DOUGLAS AND MARY PERKINS   (80M)
(Opticians)

Mary and Douglas met while studying for their optician degrees at Cardiff university in the sixties. The couple went on to develop their own chain of opticians, which they sold in 1980 to run Specsavers, now Britain's largest optical retailer. Their Guernsey based firm took advantage of the influence of fashion on eyeware and the shift in the image of glasses from geeky to glamourous. In 1984, new government legislation finally allowed opticians to advertise, and for their customers to buy glasses from any opticians, which was hugely lucrative for Douglas and Mary Perkins.

They encouraged smaller opticians to incorporate their name while still retaining a stake in the business. The idea was massively successful, and now Specsavers has over four hundred outlets and is worth an estimated £70m overall.

NIGEL JAGGER AND FAMILY (71M)
(Freight and investments)

Len and Nigel Jagger, the dynamic father and son duo, live and operate from Jersey.
Nigel who is forty-nine, took an estimated £3m when he sold 'Business Age' magazine to VNU publishing. His other media interests have netted him a reasonable fortune. He also chairs CERT Group, a Hertfordshire based freight company worth around £10.5m on its net assets

Len began making his fortune as a car dealer in Yorkshire. After selling the business he bought shares in UEI then sold them in 1982.

The money from this transaction he wisely put into Atlantic Computers. When British Commonwealth took them over, Len's shares were worth £60m. Between them, Jagger & Son have around £71m on the clock.

MAURICE SEGAL AND FAMILY (60M)
(Hotels)
Maurice Segal and his family own the Modern Hotels group, based in Jersey, and Expotel Hotel Reservations (worth around £30m alone) in London.

PETER JOHNSON (£52M)
(Hampers and football)
Peter Johnson, who is based in the Channel Islands, developed the Park Hamper Company in Merseyside. The company produces mail order Christmas hampers, the popularity of which have helped to make him a multi millionaire.

MIKE BELL (52M)
(Property)
Mike Bell has stakes in property in France and shopping centres in England, which he looks after from his residence in Jersey. One property deal in the Midlands netted him at least £30m in one fell swoop: proof, if proof were needed, of his great business acumen.

IAIN SHARP (50M)
(Parcel delivery)
Iain Sharpe made his fortune by founding Target Express Parcels in Warrington. In 1998, he sold 43% of the business, netting £158m. Two years later the entire business went under the hammer for a tidy £220m,

with Sharp's cut at around £50m in total. Iain now resides in the Channel Islands.

SIR JULIAN HODGE AND FAMILY (47M)
(Finance)

It seems that Sir Julian Hodge does not wish to become any richer, and he probably won't. So many charities benefit from the open-handedness of this ninety-three year old Cardiff born financier that if he continues to give away his 'small change' this way he will no doubt stick at his current level of wealth, as he is well known as one of the most generous givers to charity in Britain

In 1997 he offered a small fortune to campaigners opposing Welsh devolution. Sir Julian also offered to donate £3m for a new Catholic Cathedral to be built in Cardiff. This was turned down as unfortunately, this would have involved building on a park. The family have a stake worth £28m in the Carlyle Trust, a Cardiff based bank with an estimates £134m of net assets in 2001.

His career in accountancy began in night school whilst he held down a day job as a railway clerk. Eventually having built up and sold three businesses, including The Commercial Bank of Wales, for £31m, Sir Julian retired to a quiet life in Jersey in 1986.

THE EARL OF JERSEY

The Earl of Jersey who, not surprisingly, lived in the Island of Jersey, had most of his money staked in several hundred acres of Osterley Park Estate in west London near Heathrow airport. This is a particularly valuable site, and the property group MEPC is working with his family trust to develop it in a tasteful and sensitive manner. The whole project is probably worth in excess of £50m.

The Earl always showed a great interest in the Jersey cow. At one time, as president of the World Jersey Cattle Bureau, he travelled extensively helping to promote the famous breed. He was also the proud owner of about £5m worth of art treasures. These gave him so much pleasure - after all, when you get to be eighty-eight years old it is nice to have something other than TV to look at! The Earl passed away in 1998 and his grandson inherited his titles and all the responsibilities. William Child-Villiers is now the 10th Earl of Jersey.

If you are twenty-two years of age and intent on following an already successful acting career, suddenly becoming Earl of Jersey, a double Viscount and a Baron can be a bit of a facer. A whole new world opens up, a world of pomp, ceremony and ritual and a seat in the House of Lords. This could be quite disconcerting and not necessarily a welcome diversion from a career on the stage.

Life for this young man will never be quite the same but at least he is blessed with an understanding family. One wonders if he regrets his ancient ancestor being awarded the earldom by King William III three hundred years ago!

LADY BUTLIN

When Sir Billy Butlin sold his string of holiday camps to Rank he gained a cool £43m. When he sadly died in 1980, he left a large part of his wealth to charity.

His widow, Lady Sheila Butlin, has carried on the tradition of kindness and generosity to charities and good causes through the Billy Butlin Trust. Lady Sheila who lives in Jersey still has around £55m in her purse.

Chapter Six
Famous Names With Island Connections

Long before William Cody was even thought of, a clairvoyant told his mother that one day she would bear a son who would become world famous. William arrived in 1846 and died in poverty in 1917 but the seventy colourful years in between proved that prediction to be amazingly accurate.

BUFFALO BILL

At the age of eleven young Bill rather blotted his copy book by whipping out his bowie knife and slashing a class-mate during a fight. That same night he shipped out as an extra hand on a wagon train. At fifteen years old he was riding the famous Pony Express and was celebrated for his three hundred and twenty two mile dash. He completed this journey in twenty-one hours of continuous riding over rough ground - him and twenty different horses.

By the time he was thirty he was chief of scouts and Indian fighter for the 5th Cavalry. Bill also hunted and killed over four thousand buffalo to supply meat for the Army and civilian workers. As this career came to an end - perhaps they ran out of buffaloes - a writer, intrigued by Bill's exploits, wrote several stories, no doubt well embellished, in which he dubbed him Buffalo Bill. This created interest in 'The Wild West.' Soon Bill Cody had a 'Wild West Rough Riders' show touring America and

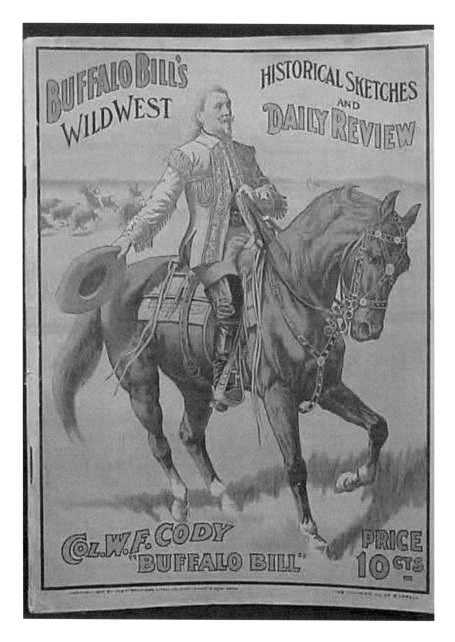

Buffalo Bill - another famous name with Channel Island links

eventually Europe. The now Colonel William F. Cody 'killed" Indians in mortal combat every night and twice on Saturdays, sometimes in a hand to hand fight.

As they had no TV in those days, all this went down very well with the audiences and soon the now famous Buffalo Bill was receiving accolades and gifts from, amongst others, Queen Victoria and other crowned heads of Europe and Russia.

Bill Cody hung up his bowie knife in 1910, stating that he was 'going home for a well earned rest.' Unfortunately his money had not stuck to him as closely as his Buffalo Bill title. He was a very caring and generous man. In the end - too generous. He died virtually penniless at his sisters home in Denver. Annie Oakley said of him: 'He was the kindest, loyalist, simplest man I ever did meet.'

The Cody Family Association in America has several thousand members, all of them being connected with or descendants of Philip Le Cody of Massachusetts. There is a museum in Cody, Wyoming and another in LeClaire where Buffalo Bill was born.

The name Cody came from Le Cody - originally Le Caudey from Jersey in the Channel Islands.

LAWRENCE OF ARABIA

Thomas Edward Lawrence was born in 1888. Twenty six years later during the 1914/18 war, he was to become Lawrence of Arabia. His technique of not only disguising himself as an Arab but virtually becoming one of them, earned him the title world-wide. In this role and with the backing of his military training, he led the Arabs against the Turks in several successful campaigns.

After leaving the Army he wrote a book, 'The Seven Pillars of Wisdom.' Later he joined the Royal Air Force.

He was killed in a motorcycle accident near Bovington Camp.

Young Tom Lawrence lived at, and no doubt played on the sands of, Havre des Pas in Jersey. He was here for a short time when his parents came over to Jersey from France for the birth of his baby brother.

SIR CHARLES SPENCER CHAPLIN KBE

Charles Chaplin was born in London on April 16, 1889. Both his parents were on the stage and he followed in their footsteps to become that beloved character whose silly walk and comical capers could have an audience rolling in the aisles. On other occasions, the pathos he could bring to the character of a down and out or a tramp would bring tears to the eyes of a tax collector.

Charlie Chaplin starred in countless films from 'The Gold Rush' and 'City Lights' to his Oscar winning 'Limelight' in 1973. He died on Christmas Day 1977.

Before his film career took off, he was with Fred Karno's Variety Company and they were booked in to play at The Opera House in Gloucester Street, for four nights from Monday August the 12th, 1912. As there was no afternoon show on the Thursday, the company decided to wander down and have a look at the Jersey 'Battle of Flowers.' Charlie, being a natural comedian, couldn't resist joining in the parade. He soon had the crowd in stitches with his clowning, but some of the organisers were not amused by this 'silly little man.' The official photographer was less than happy as, every time he tried to get a shot of the floats, Charlie popped up in the way. He pointed this out loudly and with feeling. Charlie Chaplin immediately melted back into the crowd, some of which were disappointed to see him go as 'It had been the best bit so far!'

JOAN CRAWFORD

Le Sueur (pronounced as in swer-ve) is a name well known in the Islands. Mention can be found as far back as 1638.

When Tommy Le Sueur left Jersey for Canada, it was to find work but instead he found a wife. He married Anna Ball-Johnson very soon after his arrival and they had three children. The third child, Lucille, was born on March 23rd 1908 in the poorer side of San Antonio in Texas. As a youngster she took up dancing lessons. She progressed well and, in 1923 she went on the boards professionally - became a full time hoofer, as they might have said!

Lucille, who had taken her step-father's name, Cassin, was in the chorus of a Broadway review when, in 1925, she was spotted by a talent scout. This lead to an MGM contract. She was in three films before MGM changed her name to Joan Crawford, a name dreamed up in a movie magazine competition.

Her first talkie, 'Untamed,' was in 1929. She made more than one hundred films, including, 'Whatever Happened to Baby Jane.' She was involved in writing five books and was featured in more than thirty books and publications. Despite all this activity, Joan Crawford found time to marry four husbands including Douglas Fairbanks, Jr. She also adopted four children.

Her last performance was in 1970 as Dr Bruckton in 'Trog.'

Lucille died in New York on May the 13th, 1977.

KENNETH MORE

Kenneth More, much beloved by film audiences, was born in Buckinghamshire in September 1914. He attended school in Sussex, but his connection with Jersey was his education at Victoria College.

In the early thirties he was a fur trapper in Canada. Later he worked briefly for an engineering firm. His warmest memories, however, were of the times when he worked behind the scenes at the famous London Windmill Theatre, celebrated for it's nude revues.

Kenny did 'bit' parts and comedy sketches as well as work back stage. In this way he learned his trade, and later played in repertory all over England.

His first film, 'Look up and Laugh' was screened in 1936.
He spent the war years with the Royal Navy as a Lieutenant, then returned to his acting career.

Kenny appeared in more than forty films, including the unforgettable 'Genevieve.' He wrote three books, married three times and had two daughters. His eventful life ended when he died in London aged sixty-eight.

JACQUELINE DU PRE

Jacqueline was born in Oxford in 1945 and 'took up' the cello at the age of five, first at The London Cello School, then later at The Guildhall School of Music, with William Pleeth. By now she was considered a prodigy and went on to study in Paris, Switzerland and Moscow.

Her recording of the Elgar concerto won her the Queen's prize in 1960 and she made her debut as a concert cellist at the Wigmore hall – aged just sixteen!

There was great excitement when during the early sixties, one of the greatest cellists in the world performed at Jersey's West Park Pavillion. Jaqueline du Pre's incomparable renditions of Bach and Elgar were acclaimed world wide in those days. The fact that Arthur Lobb, well known in the Island's musical circles, was able to arrange for such a sort after celebrity to play locally may be partially due to her local connections. The name du Pré, or Dupre is local and she often visited the Island, usually staying in a cottage at Arhirondel, in Gorey. While here she also gave a concert at Victoria College for hopeful young musicians.

Jacqueline was also soloist at the London, Bath and Edinburgh Festivals. She was with the BBC Symphony Orchestra when they toured the USSR. She also toured North America and Canada where she played at the World Fair. At the age of twenty-two, she married conductor Daniel Barenboim. Occasionally Jacquelne was the soloist at her husband's concerts.

In 1972 her career was brought to an end by the cruel blow of multiple sclerosis. Bravely she took to teaching and did a series of televised Master Classes. It is rather uncanny that at the age of nine, she told her family that when she grew up she wouldn't be able to walk or move! Jacqueline du Pré died in October 1987 aged forty- two.

Jacqueline received several awards including The Musician of the Year of 1975. Incorporated Society of Musicians 1980 and four years later Honorary Fellowship of St. Hilda's College but of course the presentation of the OBE in 1976 was the highlight of her career.

The book 'A Genius in the Family,' written by her sister Hilary and brother Piers, was published in 1997 and the film 'Hilary and Jackie' was released in Britain in January 1999.

The world famous Jersey cow

Chapter Seven
Famous Exports

The distinctive doe-eyed Jersey cow, so like a deer in some respects, is thought to originate from Egypt or North Africa. The Zebu which had held rank in the Indus Valley were of similar build and were noted for their fine skin texture and very rich milk. It is thought that their offspring were sent to Egypt where they were crossed with the local breeds.

THE JERSEY COW

The Zebu, like the Jersey, was a mild mannered lady, only spurred to anger when protecting her young. She is not to be confused with the great wild ox of that period, which was alleged to be 'near the size of an elephant, very fast and very fierce' - and no one tried milking them. Eventually they migrated and as they mixed with other breeds, they would have lost their hump. One will see cattle elsewhere that bear a resemblance, but for several reasons, Jerseys, once described as 'the Arab of the bovine world,' are the finest in the world.

Jersey cows are famous for their rich milk and the Channel Island milk which arrives in bottles on many an English doorstep is in fact mostly from Jersey herds, especially the 'gold top.' The Jersey is exported all over the world, and although she is no stranger in foreign parts, no cow or bull of any breed is allowed to be brought into the Island.

This is in order to keep the breed pure.

A law on the import of 'strangers' came about as early as 1763 but a total ban was made law in 1826 when it was discovered that certain cunning individuals were bringing cattle in from France then, a few days later, exporting them to England as 'Jerseys'!

The only time when this law could not operate was during the Occupation between 1940 and 1945 when large, black and white French cows were brought in by the Germans. Although these were purely for the Army meat ration there was nearly a disaster.

The story goes that one day a farmer was looking out of his window when he saw a German soldier coming up the road with one of these large beasts in tow. As he gazed in amazement the farmer saw them about to enter his field. Moving as fast as only a Jersey farmer can when his heritage is at risk, he was out of the door in seconds and stopped them in their tracks. The explanation in broken English that this cow was on heat and he was taking it to the nearest bull, caused alarm bells and telephone bells to ring across the Island.

The Head of The Jersey Agriculture Department. telephoned the German Commandant at his HQ in College House and explained the seriousness of the problem. The outcome was that the German soldier and his frustrated companion were sent sadly on their way. The breed was safe. Strangely, it was the German order that a number of cows be slaughtered for meat each week that ensured the high quality of the breed post war.

The German authorities stated the number of cattle to be slaughtered, but left the selection to the Committee of Agriculture. Using a points system and with the co-operation of the farmers, who would sometimes do a swap with a neighbour, they made sure that the finest animals stayed safe in their two fields.

Naturally the cow population was getting somewhat depleted. Then, just to add to the problems, towards the end of the Occupation they ordered three hundred animals to be sent to Alderney 'on the hoof.' However, there was deep joy in Alderney when, in 1945, two bulls were sent over for a happy reunion with those deported Jerseys.

The period following the war heralded an unprecedented demand for Island cattle. In 1948 over two thousand found new homes across the world. In 1989 a cow called 'Daydream 225' was sold in auction for a record 3000 guineas but that record was broken and a new British one established in 1995 when Mr J.P.Le Ruez sold 'Supreme Vedas Designett" for 4000 guineas (£4200).

The Jersey cow population at this time stood at 3748 - possibly less the twenty-nine who were off to Qatar. By air! Up to 1950 the thousands of Jerseys exported, mainly to America, had travelled by boat but then, as the more up to date method became popular, more and more animals took to the skies.

The World Jersey Cattle Bureau which was formed in 1921 is a global organisation covering more than twenty seven countries. Their aim is to safeguard the interests of the breed, generate research and dispense information. The Bureau encourages, promotes and endeavours to improve the Jersey breed world-wide.

And finally, have you ever wondered why, in wet weather, you may see the cows in Jersey wearing a kind of tarpaulin coat? Ask any farmer, he will tell you. It's to keep the rain out of the milk!

THE JERSEY ROYAL
The potato came to Europe in 1585. Sir John Hawkins and later Sir Walter Raleigh had found them in Equador and Chile where the local Indians grew them in the moist leaf mould of the forest floor.

Soon many countries including Ireland began to experiment with crops of these unusual 'apples of the earth.' It is curious that today the Americans often refer to them as the 'Irish potato.'

They started to catch on in Jersey around 1772 but only in a small, 'just for fun' way. Gradually interest and crop sizes increased till, during August and September 1807, Jersey exported six hundred tons of maincrop potatoes. Exports increased each year, then came trouble. The blight of 1845 followed by several bad winters almost ruined the trade - and the farmers.

It was about this time that St Ouens Farmer, John Le Caudey came up with the idea that if they planted on the warmer, south facing, cotils (sloping fields) and used a lot of guano as fertiliser, they might just get a crop of potatoes early - perhaps April or May time, and thus beat everyone else to it. He encouraged the farming community to have a go, opened up his own store for packing and organised the export of the 'earlies.' The first basketful reached the London market in April 1859.It was the start of the 'potato season' as we know it. Within five seasons the quantity exported had risen to four thousand tons. The grateful farmers and merchants presented John Le Caudey with an illuminated address, 150 sovereigns and a gold watch.

In 1880 Hugh De La Haye, a well known Jersey farmer, was visiting Le Caudey's store when he was given, as a curiosity, a very large potato with sixteen eyes.

Taking it home, Hugh cut it into pieces and planted them on his land. The result was a mixture of kidney shaped and round potatoes with a very distinctive taste.

Proudly, he exhibited his first basketful and they were dubbed 'The Royal Jersey Fluke' by the editor of the local paper. The export of the Early Jersey Royals began in 1884.
Within ten years the tonnage had risen to nearly seventy thousand tons. As the Royals became increasingly popular, it was felt that quality controls should be put into effect. Over the years these became quite strict and, though not always popular in some quarters, they served to maintain the standard and taste of the Royal potato.

Over the years the decline in the number of farms and increased competition from abroad caused potato exports to decrease. In 1998 a little under forty thousand tons were shipped to the English market.

In June 1940 the Occupation of the Islands coincided with the height of the potato season. Not wanting to waste this precious food, someone had the bright idea of putting several hundreds of tons into storage in Commercial Buildings. It wasn't long before nature took it's course. As 'meltdown' started, an unpleasant brown liquid began to seep slowly out under the doors of the warehouse, across the pavement and along the gutters. The smell was appalling and in no time the entire district was infested with billions of tiny flies. The humble spud had struck back!

THE GUERNSEY TOMATO

The growing of 'toms' in heated glasshouses was actually going on in 1792, but then it was only the gentry who enjoyed this privilege.

By 1830, Guernsey had more 'glass' than anywhere else in Europe.

Ten years later it was said: 'there are glasshouses being built for profit by everyone, even persons little above the class of cottages.' If such a snobbish remark were overheard by a good Guernseyman today, the speaker could be sure of receiving a ripe Guernsey tom behind the ear.

With three quarters of Guernsey's growing area under glass, the introduction in 1861 of a regular steamer run to the United Kingdom provided a great boost to tomato export. 1861 saw just three tons of these 'love apples,' as they were known in some circles, leave the Island.

It took just one hundred years for that figure to rise to 6,000 tons of Guernsey tomatoes exported annually to the United Kingdom.

The popularity of the Guernsey tomato continued to increase until a seasonal record of over fifty thousand tons left the Island. Unfortunately, this export has slowly lessened till the figure for 1998 was a little over three thousand tons. Happily though, the export of flowers is flourishing. Most of them are grown under the glass that was abandoned by the 'tom.'

JERSEYS, GUERNSEYS AND HOSIERY

In 1600 there were quite a few sheep gamboling about in Jersey and Guernsey. The wily Channel Islander knew that sheep meant fleece and that fleece, with the aid of a spinning wheel, becomes wool - and there lies profit.

The names 'jersey' and 'guernsey' actually refers to the type of yarn used. However, as the jumpers originated in the Islands, the names have stuck.

The jerseys and guernseys were knitted by the fishermen and their families with the intention of producing a good, snug-fitting, 'Atlantic gale proof' jumper. It was knitted 'on the round,' like a stocking - and using four needles. The neck was 'so tight, as to make the ears bleed' and there were no gaps or fastenings to catch in the fishing gear. The jersey usually had a distinctive anchor knitted into the pattern.

Actually, the patterns varied according to the whim of individual knitters, and there were hundreds of them. Dotted across the UK from Scotland to Cornwall, wives were busily clicking away, manufacturing these jumpers for the 'men that go down to the sea.'

In Scotland they tended to be called 'garnseys' - needles were known as wires. So, although they were originally made locally, the jumpers were not the main export - it was knitted stockings! Today, guernseys and jerseys are made in their respective Islands using more modern methods.

The knitting trade which was all the rage in Europe began to take off in Jersey with the knitting of stockings or hose. Soon it became Jersey's second major industry with entire families throughout the island staying at home, singing and telling stories. It was whispered that some women even knitted on Sundays!

As many as six thousand pairs of stockings were being exported to France each week - and wool was having to be imported urgently! The trouble was, the harvests were not being harvested and the precious vraic, (seaweed, used to fertilise crops) was being left to rot - and smell on the beaches. The authorities soon got wind of this and were, naturally, most concerned. The farms could not be allowed to go to rack and ruin but, on the other hand, they recognised the importance of the knitted exports.

They issued two decrees. There was to be no knitting during harvest time and the vraic was to be collected without further to do and spread on the land. This under pain of a bread and water diet in the local cooler. The second decree was aimed at keeping up the quality of the product. In future only three ply yarn was to be used - any existing two ply was confiscated.

The Jersey hose became famous throughout Europe, even as far as Italy. It was thought to be superior to silk as the latter tended to shrink and rot. When Mary Queen of Scots approached the executioner's block she was wearing 'a pair of Jersey hose white.' Let it be hoped that they gave the poor lady some comfort.

Chapter Eight
Did You Know?

If you decided to take on 'The Atlantic Challenge' and row 3, 046 miles from Tenerife to Barbados you would need to take a friend along. If after only a few days out your mate did his back in and had to be taken off, it would be very tempting to jump ship and thumb a lift.

However, with only about 3,000 miles more to go, thirty-five year old John Searson, made of sterner stuff than most of us, just carried on rowing and rowing. And rowing – for fifty nine days. Actually breaking the record for a solo Atlantic crossing.

THE ATLANTIC CHALLENGE
Entering 'The Atlantic Challenge' was a challenge in itself. Two years of planing, approaching businesses and organisations for sponsorship, and of course not forgetting to apply for three months off from work at the Jersey Met. Office! Whilst some businesses thought the whole thing too risky many more offered their support and encouragement.

When John and his rowing partner, Dr Carl Clinton set out it was with high hopes and a determination not to let down their friends, well-wishers and sponsors. In the end, it was those very people who helped John to keep going.
After Carl's back injury put him out of the race, John Searson was suddenly a very small lonely dot in a very big ocean. It was then that mental toughness became as important as physical strength.

The flood of encouraging messages by e-mail and satellite phone from friends, relatives, colleagues, youngsters from his old school, Grand Vaux and even strangers world-wide helped so much to keep him going, particularly at times when his spirits were at low ebb.

One message which particularly impressed John came from one of the New Zealand team who had finished in first place. It was simply: 'Pain fades quickly, pride lasts forever.' That message was proved right as, rowing strongly, John finally approached Barbados and saw his girlfriend Abigail and his friend Carl on the first boat coming out to meet him.

It is disappointing that his fantastic effort cannot stand as a solo record because he started out double crewed with Carl. The existing solo record stands at 99 days – so John Searson's 59 days and 12 hours rather speaks for itself!

THE STATES

'The States?' our visitors ask us - 'What exactly is that?' Well might they ask for 'The States' comes from the French 'Etats' and refers to those sections of Island life that, before 1948, were responsible for governing Jersey. These states, or stations in life, used to be represented by the jurats (the legal system); the rectors of the 12 parish churches (the church); and the constables and deputies (the parishes).

Since 1948, however, the Island has been governed by representatives of just three different sections of Island life. There are 12 Senators elected by all the Islanders to represent the interests of the whole Island; and 12 Constables who, with 29 Deputies, serve the interests of the individual Parish that elected them. These make a total of 53 States Members - our equivalent of the UK's MPs.

These 53 States Members, though, are not as most M.P.s are, affiliated to political parties. They serve as individuals in the States, from 3-6 years

The States Building and Chamber (inset) is situated in Jersey's historic Royal Square

The Bailiff of Jersey presides during the 'passing of keys' ceremony in 1996, when the British government handed over ownership of its castles to the Island's authorities.

under the presidency of the Bailiff who is also president of the Royal Court, the Island's highest court of Justice. They also serve as member or president, of different States committees, such as Education, Finance, Social Security and Tourism. Any policies, however, that these committees draw up and wish to carry out must first be approved by the whole of the States Assembly. If a majority of States Members vote for the Committee's suggestions, these are then implemented by the Island's civil servants.

To run their parishes, the constables are helped by their honorary police. They are the elected centeniers, vingteniers and constables officers, the number of which will depend on the size of the their parish. Then, just as the States have the attorney-general and the solicitor-general to advise them on the legality of their proposals for the Island's welfare, the constable has a 'procureur du bien public.' This procureur keeps an eye on the parish finances, as well as advising on any legal matter affecting parish life.

So, all in all, we Islanders can boast to our visitors that, since the time of King John, Jersey has always had Home Rule. Its internal affairs have never been administered from Westminster. Only its foreign affairs, such as its relationship with Europe, are dealt with by the Queen and her Privy Council. Even then, though, Jersey has been able to go its own way. Unlike the U.K., the Island is not a member of the E.U. It has negotiated the free movement of its goods throughout the E.U. but, it is not subject to the burden of all the legislation issuing forth daily from Brussels.

THE FINANCE INDUSTRY

When Hill Samuel arrived in Jersey in 1961 they were the one and only merchant bank in the island, but they were the start of something big. Nearly forty years later, Hill Samuel is just one of nearly eighty merchant banks eager to look after your savings and invest your nest egg.

Finance now accounts for more than twice the revenue produced by tourism

Despite increasing competition, Jersey has been described as one of the world's leading offshore financial centres. It employs around ten thousand people to take care of your ninety six and a half billion pound deposits plus investments of over thirty five billion.

The reason the industry is so successful - it accounts for over half the Island's income, can be put down to two factors. Firstly, extensive marketing and PR have been important in selling these services abroad and gaining the confidence of investors world-wide. Secondly, whilst the finance industry insists on total confidentiality to protect their law abiding investors, they have, at the same time, always been determined to remain squeaky clean when money laundering is suspected.

Although this has been a constant policy it has not always been easy to administer but, it seems, life is now to be made even more difficult. A new 1aw is about to be introduced which will hold them totally responsible if a 'wrong un' slips through the net with a fistful of filthy lucre. It is attempting to turn bankers into unpaid but accountable policemen.

At the time of writing, this 'proceeds of crime' law already includes nearly one hundred articles and is indeed a weighty tome to plough through.

Another problem about to beset the besieged banker is yet more legislation which will mean obtaining a licence if there is need to employ anyone who has not been a resident in the Island for five years. There are certain exceptions such as temps covering sickness and so on, but it is still going to put extra, and sometimes unwanted, pressure on existing staff. The reason for all this is that over the years, as business has expanded, merchant banks have had to rely on bringing experienced staff in from the mainland in increasing numbers so that now Jersey is bursting with bankers. The finance industry appear to be a victim of its own success!

Over the years it seems that every time some outside influence has initially caused some concern, the Jersey finance industry has been able to turn the situation to its advantage and add it to what is already a remarkable success story. Anyone who can increase their fund management from six billion to thirty six billion in eight years must be doing something right!

RESIDENTIAL QUALIFICATIONS

There are three ways of becoming a resident of Jersey apart from being born in the Island. The first is to arrive, live in bed-sit land for ten years, then apply for your 'quallies.'

If you are more brilliant at something than anyone else, you can be Essentially Employed. If you can do this for ten years you can then put in your application. The catch is that the 'Essential' status contracts usually only last three to five years - clever or what?

Last but not least is the 1(1)k regulation which opens the door to the rich and famous. This does not mean that a red carpet will appear automatically if you rattle a few coins in your pocket and smile ingratiatingly, but it helps - an income of about £750,000 p.a. will help even more!

The main question to be asked would be, will the potential resident be an economic or social benefit to the island? That is, would they pay plenty of tax, on going - ideally, around £150,000? Would they contribute to the wellbeing of the Island? Will there be a demand for extra housing for their children in the far future? What is their business and personal background? - Al Capone need not apply!

Even if the door then swings open, they haven't yet got a roof over their well groomed heads. The property they buy must be approved, and well above the price range of the average local home buyer - probably in excess of £760,000. While awaiting a decision, don't sign any property deals, or even blink an eyelid, until you get permission IN WRITING from the Housing Committee.

If you are thinking of settling in Guernsey, while there is no 1(1) k regulation as such, the housing laws - which do differ from those of Jersey, still aim to achieve the same object: 'to prevent further aggravation of the housing shortage.' There is a list of properties on the 'open list' which are available for purchase or rent. These will be all over the quarter million pound mark and although you may buy it, you might not always have the right to live in it!

AND FINALLY...

People from outside the Islands tend to view them through a variety of spectacles, ranging from rose-tinted to 'through a glass darkly!' Devotees of the 'Bergerac series will probably comment: 'There's a lot of crime there, real little den of iniquity. Beaches look good though.'

There are others who 'know' all about the Islands' offshore banking facilities and the small contingent of resident millionaires. These pundits will decide that the Islands provide a home for a load of Arthur Daleys, all living on their ill-gotten gains off the backs of British tax payers. British politicians will regularly have a go along the same lines - but only because it gets their names in the paper.

On the other hand, there are many who see the Channel Islands as a place of sea, sand and saunters through country lanes. The younger element may be drawn by beaches, surfing and other opportunities to enjoy themselves.

So where does the truth lie?

This book set out to try and answer that question. You have read a little of our history and our constitution, you know about some of the manor houses and we have introduced you to some rich and famous residents, past and present. We have even let you taste some of our famous exports - but the question remains - 'Who are we?'

Briefly, we live in exceedingly pleasant islands and we are very proud of them. We work for a living and, with luck, we can afford to take holidays away from our rock occasionally.

We are hopefully just a lottery ticket away from being rich and famous! And finally - we live in and not on these sainted Isles.

The classic status symbol - the Rolls Royce - makes a not infrequent appearance on the Islands' roads

Sources and acknowledgments

Jersey Farmers Trading Union
Royal Jersey Agricultural and Horticultural Society
Guernsey Agricultural Society
Cody Family Association
Citizen's Advice Bureau
The staff of the Jersey Library
Jersey Harbour Office

Sunday Times
Jersey Evening Post
Jersey Now
Expressions of Jersey
Who's Who
Who Was Who
Who's Who in the Channel Islands

Elizabeth Le Ruez
K.P. Durtnall
Roy McLoughlin
Rosalie Le Caudey
Derek Frigot of JISEX International